Praise for *Unvai*

"*Unvarnished Faith* is a story of faith, gratitude, and discernment. In this book, Bill intently demonstrates God's centrality in our lives and, more importantly, how we find God in our relationships and encounters with one another. It's an account of his faith journey from a passive bystander to an engaged and willing participant and the enormous gratitude he feels for the moments seemingly big and small, significant and insignificant that define that journey. The book calls us to examine our faith journeys through the lens of God and others. It is a challenge all of us need to encounter."

—REV. PETER M. DONOHUE, OSA, PHD, President of Villanova University

"In *Unvarnished Faith*, Bill reminds us that we're all connected to an experience greater than ourselves and that the path to true meaning in life is through our relationships with others. This engaging and eye-opening narrative of his mission in Nicaragua will inspire you to live your best life as well as give you a framework for taking the first step in that direction."

—DOUGLAS BRUNT, *New York Times* best-selling author, host of *Dedicated* podcast

"Bill Yoh offers readers the gift of a glimpse into a human life changed. But more than that, he reveals the crucial desire of every human being all over the world: to be loved and to love. As you engage with his particular story, you will reflect on your own journey while remembering and giving thanks for the universal story of God's love for every person. This book will pour refreshing water on the roots of your faith."

—REV. DR. LUKE A. POWERY, Dean of the Chapel, Duke University

"In the modern world, we need more healers and contributors to humanity. This book is an inspiration to anyone looking to serve others as they navigate their spiritual journeys. All the best to the readers who are looking for ways to please the Almighty by being a person of service, mercy, and love."

—FAZAL SYED, Islamic Society of Greater Valley Forge

"I am so excited for you to read this book! Bill's life was transformed in a powerful way when he accepted the responsibility that all believers have to love their neighbors as themselves. *Unvarnished Faith* is a book that reminds us of the gospel in its simplest form. I know that your spirit will be challenged and your heart refined as you read through Bill's life-changing testimony."

—JORDAN HICKS, Campus Pastor, Elevation Church

"All of us are naturally drawn to being a part of something greater than ourselves and leaving a lasting legacy with our time, talents, and treasure. *Unvarnished Faith* is a heartfelt call to action to realize that goal. You will learn how to succeed in your own God-given destiny—a destiny that includes people from near and far—by reading Bill Yoh's masterfully written, grace-filled narrative of going on a short-term missionary journey to Nicaragua. *Unvarnished Faith* will enable you to discern the divine imprint on each person and understand your unique calling to bring about gradual, eternal change—both in their lives and yours."

—DAVID JOANNES, Founder and CEO of Within Reach Global,
author of *The Mind of a Missionary*

"In *Unvarnished Faith*, Bill shares some of his experiences and Godly insights into a life connected to God and to God's people. It is touching; it is humorous; it is gripping; and it is inspiring. I can think of few books that capture the life we are called to live as Christians and invite you to read it and be changed."

—REV. W. FRANK ALLEN, Rector, St. David's Episcopal Church

"*Unvarnished Faith* inspires readers to thoughtfully consider their purpose and mission in life and tangibly demonstrates the power of faith and service in our lives."

—DAVID MORALES, author of *American Familia: A Memoir of Perseverance*

"When we look into the eyes of one another and see the face of Christ, we begin to glimpse the Kingdom of God. Bill Yoh takes us on a journey of beauty and discovery to awaken the importance of relationships. It starts with Jesus and then opens our hearts to all those we meet on the way. He is a blessed and inspiring guide."

—RT. REV. DANIEL G. P. GUTIÉRREZ,
XVI Bishop of the Episcopal Diocese of Pennsylvania

"*Unvarnished Faith* is a book about how a man's life and heart is unexpectedly transformed by a week-long trip to a foreign country. But you will find nothing 'foreign' about Bill Yoh's search for faith, meaning, and authenticity. You will be moved by the openness of one person's willingness to be changed . . . and after reading this account, you may well be changed yourself."

—FATHER EDWARD L. BECK, CNN religion commentator,
priest, author, playwright

"If like Bill Yoh you have been blessed with leadership skills, a measure of success, and a deep longing for your life to really count for something well beyond just your own comfort, *Unvarnished Faith* provides a pathway for you wrapped in an entertaining yet disruptive story. Grab a pen and dive it, expecting to discover more about your own longings to make your next season filled with meaning, joy, and impact."

—**LLOYD REEB**, Founding Partner, The Halftime Institute

"The Yoh family has a long history of servant living. I say servant living because this is what it takes to love and impact a nation. This is the story of how one such family has made and continues to make a difference in the hearts and lives of the people of Nicaragua."

—**MARK SZYMANSKI**, Regional Leader, United World Mission

"Powerful and deeply moving, Bill Yoh's *Unvarnished Faith* shares the transformative story of his mission trip to Nicaragua. In six short days, he and the teens on the trip learned lifelong lessons of shared humanity, faith in Christ, gratitude, and the healing power of positive relationships."

—**JOHN KAITES**, author of *In the Beginning*, pastor, entrepreneur, former state senator

"As a lifelong missionary and Executive Director for Latin America with a global organization, I have witnessed firsthand the difference that missions like the one described in *Unvarnished Faith* make. Delivering food and spreading hope to children and families who live in poverty is a wonderful example of what Jesus told us to do: 'Let your light shine so people see your good works and glorify God.' Bill Yoh's story highlights the reciprocal nature of missionary work and the powerful impact of human connection to broaden both your worldview and your faith."

—**DAVID SOUTHWELL**, Executive Director for Latin America and the Caribbean (retired), Association of Baptists for World Evangelism

Also by Bill Yoh

Our Way: The Life Story of Spike Yoh

UNVARNISHED
FAITH

Learning to Love with a Servant's Heart

BILL YOH

RIVER GROVE
BOOKS

This book is a memoir reflecting the author's present recollections of experiences over time. Its story and its words are the author's alone. Some details and characteristics may be changed, some events may be compressed, and some dialogue may be recreated. Some names and identifying characteristics of persons referenced in this book, as well as identifying places, have been changed to protect the privacy of the individuals and their families.

Published by River Grove Books
Austin, TX
www.rivergrovebooks.com

Distributed by River Grove Books

Design and composition by Greenleaf Book Group
Cover design by Greenleaf Book Group

Unless noted otherwise, scripture texts are taken from the *New American Bible, revised edition* © 2010, 1991, 1986, 1970 Confraternity of Christian Doctrine, Inc., Washington, D.C.

Scripture texts marked NIV are from The Holy Bible, New International Version®, NIV® Copyright © 1973, 1978, 1984, 2011 by Biblica, Inc.® Used by permission. All rights reserved worldwide.

Scripture texts marked ESV are from the ESV® Bible (The Holy Bible, English Standard Version®), copyright © 2001 by Crossway, a publishing ministry of Good News Publishers. Used by permission. All rights reserved.

Publisher's Cataloging-in-Publication data is available.

Print ISBN: 978-1-63299-637-4

eBook ISBN: 978-1-63299-638-1

First Edition

To Kelly,
The simplicity and profundity of God's love

"We and all creation are the creatures of love. We are made by love, we are marked by love, and we are made for love."

—DESMOND TUTU

Contents

Prologue

The first thing I noticed was the buzzards circling overhead. As they rose and fell among the thermal updrafts high above the tropical forest, their synchronized flight patterns were reminiscent of skywriters, only without the vapor trails forming patriotic slogans or marriage proposals.

We bounced along the winding two-lane highway, standing in the flatbed of the large, open-air cage truck, girded by steel bars providing copious airflow and ostensible safety. I held onto the bars, along with the other four American chaperones and about as many local guides, while most of the North Carolina high school students sat on the single layer of cardboard boxes of food we would soon deliver. Other trucks and smaller cars whizzed past us on the narrow, shoulderless road, but I was gaining confidence in our driver as he kept us in our lane.

Dust gritted between my teeth and adhered to the sunscreen I had applied earlier in a feeble attempt to allow the lotion to absorb before I started sweating in the Central American heat. My khaki hat's circular brim provided much-needed protection from the midmorning sun's already oppressive warmth. With the vultures up to our left, a beautiful lake emerged to our right, the far end of which was framed by a *Jurassic Park*–worthy volcano. Gathered around its summit was the slightest patch of dense white clouds, stark against blue sky.

We were approaching a trash dump near Lake Managua, where we would distribute food and spend time with the locals, some of whom lived around the perimeter and some inside the dump itself. I could not fathom how people could live in such a place, and this incomprehensibility enhanced both my curiosity and my anxiety. I lurched forward as the driver downshifted and applied the brakes. Near the entrance to the site, on the left-hand side of the road, a few familiar-looking men stood next to a souped-up black Toyota Hilux pickup and waved us over.

As we swung into the wide entryway, I noticed a small ground fire immediately inside the fence line; no one tended it or even seemed to care it was burning. Larger fires burned up ahead, some more visible than others through the low-hanging branches of the tall, broad-leafed trees. The truck stopped, and the door of our cage enclosure swung open. A man on the ground rotated a black ladder into place, the steel-on-steel clang startling a yellow cat lurking a few yards away. One by one, we flatbed riders disembarked, some descending the ladder face out, others—including cautious me—facing in and grabbing the rungs. The guides who had stood with us offloaded the food, and a stocky local man shouted semicomprehensible instructions, my once-fluent Spanish still rusty given that I had been in Nicaragua barely twelve hours. We made our way up a short hill to a flat, shaded area. My eyes kept returning to the fires up ahead.

The first person I noticed inside was a thin boy, no more than five years old, squatting on the leaf-covered ground next to a tree, his round, dark eyes taking us in, his brown face covered in soot. Beyond him, up the incline, two dozen or so kids and adults stood in the shaded protection of the trees' dense canopy. We Americans wore matching red T-shirts, while our Nicaraguan guides had on purple, allowing everyone to know who was in charge.

As we gathered near the local group, one of our leaders began to play a small acoustic guitar and sing, while another gave me one of several large trash bags full of smaller bags of plastic cars, figurines, and other assorted toys we had packed that morning back at the compound, ice-breaking playthings for the kids we would meet. After the first song was completed, many of the younger inhabitants queued up to receive the trinkets. As each youngster's small, dusty hands reached for one of the bags I held, we made eye contact. Sometimes, the children would crack a smile, the line of teeth stark against their skin. Other times, they would avert their gaze, typical childhood shyness, particularly in front of a six-foot-three American who had played nine years of football in school and still carried the weight to prove it.

Once my bag was empty, I looked for a trash can; the bag was torn in several spots. After turning left and right, I had the bizarre realization that there were no trash *cans*; I was in a trash *dump*. I dropped it on a pile of other trash beyond where everyone stood.

Once we distributed the toys, our Spanish-speaking guides called out in bright voices for the local kids to gather around and sing a few songs, after which a young, energetic female guide said a prayer in Spanish. We then lined up to form a bucket brigade to transport the thirty-three-pound boxes of food up the hill to the gathering spot. I was told that we would typically cook the food, but in this case, given the remote location, we would just distribute the boxes for the locals to prepare later.

After the leaders ensured that each family received the appropriate amount of prepackaged rice-and-soy-based meals, we left the shaded area and made our way up the rocky driveway farther into the grounds. We passed a grove of trees on our left about fifty yards past where we had gathered, the trunks of which were connected by assorted cardboard panels, tattered sheets, and makeshift partitions. Inside these, I saw various overturned boxes and smaller cardboard pieces lined up on the dirt. Maybe this was one of the places people lived?

Eventually, the shade gave way to a treeless hilltop, perhaps a hundred yards wide. A few of the American teenagers in their red shirts found a small, flat section and started kicking a soccer ball with two local boys around eight to ten years old. Each panel of the specially manufactured "mission ball" contained a Bible passage printed in Spanish—one of the signs that ours was a Christian mission.

The clearing where we now stood was covered almost entirely by trash, garbage smashed down over time so that earth and waste were indistinguishable from each other. I looked down and noticed I was surrounded by medical waste—used syringes, torn rubber bags, stained plastic tubes. I was happy to be wearing my rugged, lace-up trail shoes rather than the broken-down flip-flops or occasional pair of never-to-decay Crocs worn by the locals fortunate not to be barefoot.

Among the maladies the inhabitants incur, serious infection is common. I heard about a sixteen-year-old girl who, a few months earlier, had stepped on a nail, causing—in our guide's words—"gangrene to eat away the flesh of her foot." The guides tended to her, putting her leg on a makeshift table and literally cutting the disease out with a knife. They said she made a full recovery.

Standing on the hilltop, I now clearly saw the fires I had noticed earlier through the tree branches—spread out piles of wood, cardboard, paper, glass, random bits of clothing, all types of metal and plastic heaped together, much of it ablaze. A few buzzards were picking at the edges of the mounds, as were a gaunt-looking cow and a few stray dogs, whose ribs were visible beneath drum-tight skin. The lake and volcano I had seen from the highway were visible from the clearing, only my vantage point was now above the trees. The foreground's canopy of lush, green treetops made the terrain even more spectacular.

It was spectacular until one of our guides said the lake was so contaminated that the water was neither potable nor swimmable. This dichotomy of visual beauty and grim reality would serve as a template for the week ahead, one that would tear at any of my prior (vacationing) experiences in tropical climes.

The smell of smoke was inescapable, piles of burning trash in all directions. The odor had a faint plastic tinge but was otherwise almost pleasant, reminiscent of childhood campfires or a summer barbeque. But then I realized something was oddly absent. There was no rancidness. Nothing spoiled filled my nose. I know what my garage trash can at home smells like when I wheel it to the curb after just a week, but here we were surrounded by acres of trash accumulated over years, if not decades, but with none of the expected olfactory offense.

Then it occurred to me. There were no half-eaten take-out meals rotting in the hot sun. No discarded rotisserie chickens with decaying meat remnants between the bones. No condiment jars with sauce still lining the inside walls. Oh, right. We were in a remote region of Nicaragua, where so little food was available, no one would dare throw much away. What a difference from my world.

Unlike the group we encountered near the entrance, the people in the clearing were mostly middle-aged men. They toiled, placing objects from the low heaps into large, white burlap bags that, once filled, stood almost as tall as they were. The leader of our local guides, an expat born and raised in North Carolina named Patrick, explained that these men would spend an entire day in the heat and humidity filling just one sack with recyclable materials, which later might earn them the equivalent of a few US dollars.

The lone female inhabitant I saw on the hilltop was a thickset woman in her mid- to late twenties standing near a lanky elderly man in a faded orange ball cap. The woman wore an open-weave knit hat, a stained white baseball undershirt with blue sleeves, and black, tight-fitting pants frayed around the cuffs. To enhance our understanding of what life was like there, Patrick gathered us together and began asking her a few questions; given our group's wide range of Spanish speaking ability, he translated. Her name was María. The older man was her father. She had been raised at the dump, and she was now raising her kids here. I assumed the cardboard structure I had seen walking up was their home.

As the brief interview wound down, Patrick asked her how she felt about living there and raising her family in those conditions. This place could not have been more different from anywhere I had ever been. There was certainly no running water or sanitation, nor health care or schooling or any apparent transportation to such resources elsewhere. Bewildered and troubled after a few hours on site, I know how I and likely every other *gringo* standing around might have answered Patrick's query about how she felt: Sad? Frustrated? Angry? Guilty? Desperate? Hopeless?

Without pause, María responded in a direct, firm voice:

"Yo estoy contenta."

I am happy.

Introduction

Life's deepest meaning is not found in accomplishments but in relationships.

—GARY CHAPMAN, *The 5 Love Languages*

R eligion, in its best form, provides the community and shelter of a big tent. Faith is about a connectedness to others and to something greater than ourselves, an acknowledgment that there is more to life than what we can explain by science, circumstance, and luck. The tallest and strongest poles in this tent are relationships and love. People are social creatures, made to interact with each other. Without meaningful relationships, our existence would not be human. The most coveted form of relationship is love, the ultimate expression of connection, compassion, and desire. Loving relationships bring significance to our lives and make our time together beautiful. This book is a tribute to relationships and love, to these bonds of humanity that are both foundational bedrock and aspirational panacea.

I am Christian. A lifelong Episcopalian, I converted to Roman

Catholicism a few years ago. This conversion was a key milestone along my faith journey. While I was called to the Catholic Church, I am equally called to the catholic church (with the lowercase *c*, meaning "universal"). I believe we Christians too often focus on the relatively few differences that separate one set of customs and interpretations from another rather than celebrating the overwhelming commonality we share. The Holy Trinity, the belief that Christ died for our sins, that we should apply our abilities and resources to help others, and that we should honor God and love our neighbor (however difficult that might be) are universal Christian ideals.

I do not mean to diminish the variations among faiths, but I believe we could do more good—making the world a better place—if we cast more light onto our vast common ground rather than our thin doctrinal divides. And while the tenets of non-Christian religions and spiritual practices vary, I believe anyone who acknowledges a higher power would agree that being a good person and making life better for those around you, key tenets of relationships and love, are desirable and necessary behaviors.

This book is for anyone who thinks about their life in this way, whether you are religious in a traditional sense, identify with a less-defined version of faith, or perhaps practice activities like yoga, meditation, and mindfulness as means of accessing forces beyond yourself. Our engagement in this quest for higher meaning and connectedness—the often invisible but palpable bonds and energies that anchor and propel our time on earth—nurtures relationships and leads to love. It was these forces that pulled me to Nicaragua and filled me with a newfound perspective on my life and an appreciation for humanity's connectedness, for our role on the earth, and for God's limitless grace.

My brother Jeff and his wife, Suzanne, founded and operate a large-scale food ministry that coordinates the packing, storing, and shipping of millions of meals for underserved communities. They send much of the food they prepare to Nicaragua, where a local organization distributes it to communities in need. A few times each year, Jeff and Suzanne take groups to Nicaragua on missions to help deliver the food and spread the Gospel of Jesus, the guiding force behind their ministry.

I turned down Jeff's invitation to join him several times, mostly because I could not see myself as a missionary, going into what I perceived would be some pretty destitute and uncomfortable places to talk about Christianity. For reasons that were not clear to me at the time, I finally agreed to go as a chaperone for a group of high schoolers who would spend a week living near the capital of Nicaragua. I saw the job as helping these teenagers, largely looking out for their safety and well-being, while they would do most of the interaction with the Nicaraguans and participate in most of the God talk. I would be supporting those who would be supporting others. Little did I know that those students—and the many locals I would meet—would help me grow profoundly as a person and as a man of faith.

The trip changed my life. It sharpened my awareness of God's love and better illuminated the path Jesus wants me to walk. It awakened a dormant curiosity about my purpose and stimulated an unattended wonder about what matters. And it compelled me to write the book you are holding. It is rather egotistical to think that my story would be of interest to others, but according to Henry David Thoreau, "I should not talk so much about myself if there were anybody else whom I knew as well." I am still getting to know who I am—and who I am meant to be.

In the chapters ahead, I hope to spark interest, introspection, and perhaps even action—or as the book of Hebrews says, "to rouse one another to love and good works." Our journey will take us into austere and poverty-stricken locales. We will experience hardship and lack in ways I did not think possible. But I will also share how my conceptions of "poverty" and "lack" had been largely based on a secular, developed-world vantage. Much of what I perceived as awful began to show up as awe-full as well. My privilege enabled me to travel to Nicaragua, but it also deluded me into thinking I knew what made people rich.

I use each day of the trip to explore the life tenets that emerged for me during the mission, spiritual grapevines springing from the rootstock of relationships and love that common faith and shared experience germinated. I recognized the importance of displaying strong character. I sensed the dignity inherent in all human beings, while discovering the talents and gifts we are each compelled to use. I grappled with finding serenity in what I can control and what I cannot. I reflected on the inevitability and importance of failure, and I returned with a heightened sense of gratitude for the blessed life I lead. My six days in Pochocuape, the village where we stayed, did all of these things in profound and memory-searing ways.

While I see life (and wrote these pages) through a Christian lens, I include concepts and opinions from myriad religious, spiritual, and secular perspectives, hopeful evidence to the book's universal themes. My intent is not to teach you anything you do not already know—relationships and love are pretty simple concepts—but maybe to have you broaden the aperture with which you view the world and perhaps be a little more intentional about how the life you lead impacts others.

I am honored you chose to spend this time with me. I hope you enjoy the trip.

Part 1

SUNDAY: CHARACTER

*A life of faith is not a life of one glorious
mountaintop experience after another . . .
but of day-in and day-out consistency.*

—OSWALD CHAMBERS,
My Utmost for His Highest

1

Brotherly Calling

As I move through my middle-age years, I have become more of a morning person, belying my younger self's ability to burn the proverbial candle at both ends. One consequence of this change is that I have fallen into the unadvisable practice of packing for trips on the morning of departure rather than the night before. After a predawn alarm on a cold January Sunday, I tiptoed around Kelly's side of the bed to the closet to retrieve my well-worn Rollaboard from the top shelf. The bag was black, but years of corporate travel had led to a gray warranty replacement handle, and my initials were printed in the monogram field—two flags to identify my bag among the flock of its species that had convened in many Jetways and baggage claim carousels over the years and time zones.

The forecast for Nicaragua was sunshine, temperatures in the eighties, and high humidity. No dressy clothes were required, so my packing consisted mostly of a few pairs of cargo shorts, socks and underwear, and a few hats. My fellow missionaries and I would receive matching T-shirts to wear each day, so the long-sleeved work-out shirt I put on was one of the few shirts I brought. At my brother's suggestion (Jeff was five years my senior and veteran of several mission trips), I packed a pair of flip-flops for the evenings; otherwise, rugged trail shoes would be my footwear for the week. Even though Nicaragua's rainy season was a few months off, I included a rolled-up rain jacket (once a Boy Scout, always a Boy Scout). I had made a CVS run to purchase first-aid supplies and over-the-counter cold remedies, plus a five-day antibiotic in case Montezuma's revenge struck; Nicaraguan water is unpotable for many foreigners, and I wanted to prepare for any inadvertent ingestion.

It felt odd not bringing my laptop bag, another appendage for me in airports and remote cities, but there would be no time for computer work, and I was told the quality of the Wi-Fi would vary. I did bring my iPad in a keyboard case so I could keep up on email without having to fat-finger my iPhone all week. I packed the tablet and a few books in a backpack. The simple yet unique combination of clothing and supplies indicated a different kind of trip was afoot.

After a kiss and hug for my slumbering bride and with the sky still dead-of-winter dark, I drove to the airport for my flight to Miami, where I would meet up with eighteen other Americans from fifteen to fifty-five years old, most of whom I had never met but all of whom had chosen to spend the first full week of the new year outside the country and outside our comfort zones. Fourteen of the group were high schoolers from Charlotte Christian School—which Jeff and Suzanne's children had attended—who elected to spend the coming week on a J-term (January) mission trip. The other four travelers, including Jeff, were my fellow chaperones.

Jeff's business career has had two major phases: working at our family business (construction, staffing, and defense services and products) for some twenty years, then blazing his own trail as a successful entrepreneur for almost twenty more. He now chairs and is the majority owner of a high-growth business specializing in home and property restoration after floods and fires. Jeff's wife, Suzanne, also grew up in a family business (industrial and technical trade publications). Starting to work part-time at ten years old, she performed both operational and support functions, culminating as the firm's legislative liaison, all the while honing her project management and writing and communications skills.

In the mid-2000s, after reading Bob Buford's *Halftime*, a must-read for any midcareer professional questioning their place in life, Jeff visited the Halftime Institute in Dallas. The book and visit inspired him to begin to migrate from the corporate *success* of the first half of his life into a phase of greater spiritual *significance* for his second half (hence the title, *Halftime*). As he shared his evolving perspective with Suzanne, their common faith grew. Jeff (like me) was raised Episcopalian, while Suzanne's family worshiped at Quaker and then Presbyterian churches. Jeff and Suzanne now consider themselves nondenominational Christians, with a strong emphasis on Bible-based theology, rather than the Bible-and-prayer-book theology that many "traditional" Protestant denominations practice. They recently completed master's degrees in Christian ministry.

In the late 2000s, they began volunteering in their hometown of Charlotte with a number of different organizations, exploring together what it meant to help others. They participated in a series of local food-packing events run by a national ministry. Wanting to work as partners and as a family (their three children were teenagers), Suzanne and Jeff melded their skills and experience and—propelled by merging their respective faith journeys—started a satellite operation for Kids Against Hunger in 2011. By 2013, they saw opportunities to improve on the food ministry cost structure and delivery model and founded their own organization, Servants

With a Heart (SWH). Based outside Charlotte, this not-for-profit humanitarian organization coordinates food-packing events at churches, schools, and other organizations and delivers the meals to food-insecure communities in the US and Latin America.

In the early years, Jeff and Suzanne ran SWH with the help of their children and their children's friends. As their nest emptied and the organization grew, they solicited management support from friends and from acquaintances they had made at packing events. Today the organization functions through a volunteer leadership team of twenty-five, has engaged over 150,000 volunteers, and has packed and delivered over twenty-two million nonperishable meals to underserved communities.

While SWH has distributed well over a million meals in the greater Charlotte area, it sends most of its food to Nicaragua. The connection to the country stems from a relationship formed during Jeff and Suzanne's initial volunteer activities; Dedrick and Nancy Brown served on the planning committee for one of the early food-packing events. Their family has a ministry, Samaritans International of Waxhaw, which distributes food, educates children, and promotes Christianity across Nicaragua. They feed eighty to a hundred thousand kids every week who would otherwise go hungry! Dedrick's brother, Patrick—whom you will get to know well—lives in Nicaragua and leads the ministry Samaritans International (not to be confused with other ministries with similar-sounding names).

After working together on the packing event, the Yohs and Browns had lunch and shared their respective thoughts about meal packing, hunger, and faith. A fast and lasting friendship was born. The two couples envisioned an organization where all proceeds raised at events would support the mission of feeding hungry children rather than some portion having to cover administrative and overhead expenses—which Jeff and Suzanne perceived to be unnecessarily high in national food ministries. To support this vision, the Browns soon agreed to provide warehouse space, trucks, forklifts, and logistics support from their regional furniture supply operation, helping SWH cover its infrastructure costs entirely from ongoing support and not from event fundraising. As a result, the ministry's cost per meal has not increased since 2011, tracking about half of the national organizations' pricing. And communities and organizations who host SWH events—where people come together and pack (minimally) tens of thousands of meals in assembly line format over a day or two—know that all of their financial support goes to the ingredients and food delivery.

It was food delivery and distribution—central components in the fight against food insecurity—that put me in the role of chaperone. On the face of it, I would be there to help the teenage volunteers get something out of the week. When I returned home six days later, however, I believe I was changed as much or more than any of the teenagers; the trip would be in many ways more impactful than any other experience throughout my five decades on earth. I would confront stark contrasts in living conditions and in the human condition. I would see my mettle tested and my faith journey accelerate. I would experience what it means to relate to others on a raw, stripped-down level, where we were open and vulnerable. I would see firsthand how light can shine only in the dark. From the shattered innocence of the Garden of Eden to the far, far away imaginary galaxies of *Star Wars*, good is not visible without the negative space of evil surrounding it. Hope's powerful wings cannot overcome the tethering weight of despair without the winds of faith to provide lift. In Pochocuape, I would see this faith challenged routinely—sometimes rewarded, sometimes tasked to endure.

As I settled into my seat on the plane, the normal boarding cadence was interrupted when the captain came on the public address system to inform us of a mechanical problem involving a fuel tank, for which we would have to deplane. Fuel tank, huh? I was a nervous flyer—unfortunate with how much I had traveled in my life—so a fuel-related issue didn't feel like the seat-back tray table in row twenty-two not working; it got my attention. We passengers collected our bags and proceeded back up the Jetway, the occasional grumble breaking the group silence.

Shortly after returning to the terminal, an airline associate informed us that the plane would be unable to fly and that we should book alternate travel plans. Anyone who has flown more than a few times can guess what ensued. Pure melee, bordering on mass hysteria. A family with two young kids despondent about possibly not getting home for school and work the next day. An international traveler holding out her ticket, looking confused. Myriad others exhibiting the irrational yet predictable the-world-may-end-if-we-don't-get-on-*THAT*-flight behavior.

From the front of the rapidly growing customer service line, I heard someone shout, "My wife and I have a couple's massage in Half Moon Bay, Jamaica, *this afternoon!* What are *you* going to do to get us there?" I don't know if I was more shocked by the oddity of the phrases or the zero-to-sixty level of exasperation sprayed toward the airline representative, who did her best to remain calm and professional amid the early-morning commotion. Two things about such situations amaze me: how difficult it must be to work as a customer-facing airline employee and how undies-in-a-bunch miserable some people get when flight delays occur. Both behaviors provide a peek of what is inside a person, those innate facets of mentality and personality that surface when life tilts off equilibrium. We get a glimpse into people's character.

Being relatively deep in the queue, I decided to call the airline's 800 number. Since it was Sunday morning, a light travel time, I got through and booked a later flight to Managua, Nicaragua's capital, via Dallas. While I did not add to the passenger frenzy, don't think I am always a saint in such situations; I have had my fair share of flight delay frustrations. However, something was different on this day. I was calm, standing patiently in line and pressing the appropriate buttons on my phone to connect to an agent. I guess knowing where I was headed and what I was going to do prompted my good traits of character to outshine my bad.

What exactly is character? Of course I am not referring to a character in a play or the character of a painting, but to the behaviors and expressions of ethos that show the world what kind of person you are. The concept is amorphous, enigmatic, and subjective. For me, the primary ingredients in this mixing bowl—and what I think about while reflecting on that long Sunday of traveling alone—are integrity, humility, and hard work.

2

Burden of Courage

Two uneventful flights later, I arrived in Managua, fourteen hours into my day but only six hours behind schedule. As the passengers in front of me starting filing off the plane, I unloaded my Rollaboard from the overhead bin and placed it in the aisle, then performed one final check of my seatback pocket (I left a flip phone in one years ago). When I stood back up, my bag had disappeared! Almost immediately, I noticed another piece of luggage similar to mine in the aisle and assumed (hoped) that someone had simply taken the wrong one. I sprinted up the Jetway and, since it was nighttime and the airport was fairly empty, quickly made my way to the point in the terminal where arriving passengers line up for processing. Much to my relief, I spotted my bag in tow behind the suitcase-mixer-upper. She was Latina (Nicaraguan, I suppose), so my long-idle Spanish was put to a quick test. Fortunately the mistake was recognized and remedied, the woman exhibiting an apologetic grace that stood in stark contrast to the outburst from Mr. Couple's Massage that morning back in Philadelphia.

I soon saw my brother Jeff through the glass wall dividing arrivers from greeters, his ever-present red beard a little thicker and grayer since I had last seen him some nine months earlier. He had arrived earlier in the day, traveling with the group from Charlotte through (my missed connection in) Miami. He sported a baseball cap and T-shirt, as well as weathered cargo shorts and well-worn sandals. He was standing next to a local-looking man I would learn was Jimmy, who worked with our host organization, Samaritans International of Nicaragua; he was one of our in-country liaisons. Jimmy also sported a T-shirt but wore blue jeans and closed-toed shoes. While not quite Jeff's height, he was stocky, with a bull's neck, full cheeks, and a thin beard connecting his sideburns to his goatee. He wore thin wire-framed glasses and, like pretty much every other man I would meet, a baseball cap. Jimmy's focused eyes and firm handshake conveyed confidence and warmth. His English, as he asked about my flight and commented on the bag mix-up, seemed strong.

I would learn later that Jimmy was packing heat, a Glock concealed under his shirt. A few of our Samaritans handlers were trained security guards who carried handguns to assure our well-being. While the US Department of State cited "low overall reported crimes" at the time of our travel, they also stated that "many crimes go unreported, and anecdotal information suggests that crime is increasing. Crimes are more frequently being conducted with weapons and violence." Samaritans International had been operating safely in Nicaragua for many years, so I was not overly concerned, but having professional, armed guides provided peace of mind.

Nicaragua, located at the geographical center of Central America, is bordered by Honduras to the north and Costa Rica to the south and spans from the Caribbean to the Pacific. Different regions were once under Spanish and British rule; the majority of its 6.3 million inhabitants live in the western, Spanish-influenced area, which includes Managua. Over 90 percent of Nicaraguans identify as Christian, although as I would experience in the days to come, many practiced their faith much differently and with far more conviction than I did. A major political, economic, and cultural influence in the country is the power and oversight of President Daniel Ortega, who first became the nation's chief executive in 1984 following the Sandinistas' government overthrow a few years earlier. Voted out of office in 1990, Ortega regained the presidency in 2006 with an ostensibly less Marxist, more democratic platform. However, he has since attained an ever-tightening grip on the government through periodic constitutional modifications to ensure his continued reign.

Nicaragua is one of the poorest countries in the world, with a GDP of less than fourteen billion dollars. More telling, its per capita GDP of just over two million dollars ranks second-to-last in the Western Hemisphere, besting only Haiti's. This is a primary reason I was meeting up with Jeff in this remote, austere location.

Exiting the airport, I was struck by the warm, soupy air still lingering long past sunset, my cheeks and exposed forearms spritzed by the humidity. Unlike airports in the States, where traffic officers keep the vehicles moving, the pickup curb was three cars deep. A major roadway passed within fifty feet of the terminal. We loaded my bags and climbed into the rugged Toyota Hilux, and off we drove to Pochocuape, a suburb of Managua and my home for the next six days.

On the nighttime drive from the airport, we passed several large, well-lit billboards featuring warm, smiling photos of President Ortega and his wife, Rosario Murillo—government-funded attempts to convey warmth but also not-so-subtle reminders that leadership was always watching. We also saw many brightly lit tree-shaped metal structures along the highway, which had piqued my curiosity on my Boeing 757's final descent, their large form and gaudy neon glow visible from thousands of feet up. Jeff explained that, as Señora Murillo had accumulated more and more power—eventually adding vice president to her first lady title—she commissioned these "Trees of Life" to beautify the capital. However, the swirly top portion of each, intended to constitute the leaves, may clandestinely form the number 666, a possible reference to witchcraft and Satan worship. I had read about spiritual warfare in places like Nicaragua. While this was my first exposure to it, it would not be my last.

We passed a large yellow sign for a fast-food restaurant called *Guapollon*, which I later learned promoted its menu as *pollo de mi barrio* (chicken from my neighborhood), indicating the owners' attempt to appear neighborly and neighborhood-y. I also heard, however, that some locals, particularly younger ones, resented the attempted connection because they didn't consider the local neighborhood that great. I remember thinking how this dynamic contrasted with my hometown—part of Philadelphia's well-to-do Main Line suburbs— where many consumers prefer and will pay a premium for locally sourced, farm-to-table fare. The differences between my world and this new one were engulfing my senses, the morning flight delay in Philadelphia already a distant memory.

As we rode along, Jeff—a strong extrovert and consummate relationship builder—brokered the introductory conversation between Jimmy and me. From this exchange and a few later one-on-one discussions, I pieced together Jimmy's bio. Now in his mid-thirties, he was one of six children. His family had fled Nicaragua for Miami, Florida, in the 1980s to escape the strife associated with the protracted civil war between the Sandistas and the Contras. I had followed this conflict distantly, usually via Peter Jennings's evening news updates, his mild, soothing Canadian accent part of my childhood predinner auditory milieu. The conflict, however, was anything but mild or soothing. The Sandinistas came to power via revolution in the late 1970s and then fought for years with the Contras—initially the preceding regime's National Guard, funded and trained in part by the United States' CIA. The associated violence compelled families like Jimmy's to flee the country.

Unable to make their way as refugees in America, the family returned to Nicaragua in the 1990s but continued to struggle. As Jimmy related, "We moved back and lost it all. No house. No food. It was very bad. I just thought there was no more hope. I couldn't see the light out of the tunnel." At age eleven, he secured his first job working in his neighborhood, and at fourteen, he started translating for American missionaries. He recalls how, before he accompanied the *norteamericanos* into a community, they would encourage him to accept Jesus Christ. "They ministered to me. I saw hope and love. I saw what a mission team can do for people who feel lost."

Now, two decades later, Jimmy had become one of the senior members of the Samaritans staff. He excelled at planning and operations, and his English was nearly flawless. His path to Christ was inspiring. Like other Samaritans employees, he wore his faith on his sleeve. Later in the week, Jimmy described an event that showed how his skill set and his faith interacted. Many years ago, he was in charge of logistics for a fifty-member mission team working in a remote village in the northern part of the country. They had brought some food with them, but most of their materials were coming separately in various trucks. The mission was organized into four groups, and on this particular day, all four experienced delays—all at once.

As Jimmy tells it, "At nine o'clock in the morning, I get the first call that the cooler of medical supplies was left back at the compound. Twenty minutes later, I learn that the pastors were not coming. Then the people with the children's Bibles call to say the Bibles are heading to the wrong village. Finally, the construction leader calls to say the materials truck broke down. For a logistics man, this is my worst nightmare. I was worried and then became overwhelmed.

"But then this tiny *abuela*, or grandmother, maybe seventy-five or eighty years old, taps me on the shoulder. *Now what?* I say to myself. As I turned around and bent over to look in her eyes, she said, 'I just want to say thank you.' I said, 'For what?' And she told me that the food we had brought would feed her family. Only then did I notice the group of relatives behind her, most of them children. That's when everything went silent for me. A total stop. I heard a voice deep in my heart say, *So you think you have problems, Jimmy?* I just couldn't come out of that moment. It was the voice of God; a miracle took place. It changed my life."

Jimmy and I both had tears in our eyes as he finished his account. I was particularly moved by someone like him—stocky and carrying a firearm—sharing something so personal to a relative stranger. But these are the type of people and the kind of stories I would encounter all week. To finish the story, by late afternoon Jimmy had sorted out the logistics issues, and all the people and materials arrived, making the trip a success.

Jimmy's dedication to his vocation, along with the candor with which he shared his life experience, depict the first aspect of character for me—integrity. A former colleague and mentor of mine liked to say, "Integrity carries the burden of courage." Jimmy's abuela-induced epiphany showed honesty, transparency, and courage. His godly experience in that northern community is what Christians call "a mountaintop moment," harkening to when Moses ascended Mount Sinai to converse with God and receive his marching orders for the chosen people, including the Ten Commandments. These moments of clarity and invigoration and growth are few and far between. And they are often not square-in-your-face but instead are like the gentle whisper in which the Old Testament prophet Elijah senses the presence of God.

As a young adult, I partook in a series of personal development programs known as the Curriculum for Living by Landmark Worldwide, which grew out of the 1970s philosophies of Werner Erhard and his controversial Erhard Seminars Training (EST). Despite the common belief that EST and Landmark were cultish fads, I found the coursework enlightening as a recent college grad embarking on adult life. Similar to Christianity's mountaintop moment concept, Landmark talked about windows of possibility, how people could see ways to accomplish difficult tasks, connect with others in authentic ways, or experience a heightened awareness of their surroundings, but only for brief periods of time. The key is how one acts—and interacts—during those epiphanies.

The integrity I saw in Jimmy—which was corroborated by Patrick, his boss; his coworkers; and my brother, who had known him for years—helped define his growth, both as a man of God and professionally. Starting as a teenage translator, and then becoming a logistics coordinator, he was now running multiple mission teams simultaneously, the second-in-command of Samaritans International and their hundreds of feeding centers across Nicaragua. His career progression illustrated how God constantly raises the bar for us Christians, presenting challenges for us to overcome and from which to grow. "Affliction produces endurance, and endurance, proven character, and proven character, hope" (Romans 5:3–4).

I gleaned a related nugget about integrity from my father, an ethical business leader but also a consummate mechanical engineer who used logic and practicality as behavioral guideposts. He always advised keeping life simple, that if you always tell the truth, you never have to worry about what you said, to whom, and when. I rephrase this counsel as *if your story is the same, your story is the same.*

Back to our evening commute, about two-thirds of the way into the twenty-kilometer trip from the airport on the eastern side of Managua to Pochocuape in the southwest, Jimmy pulled the truck into an empty parking lot of a closed, run-down strip mall. A few of the storefronts were boarded up; others looked like their best days had been decades ago. The pot-holed ground was littered with torn cardboard boxes, empty booze bottles, and random articles of dirty clothing. Jeff opened his door and said, "Let's go."

Um. Go where? We were sort of in the middle of nowhere . . . and this place was kinda creepy. But he is my big brother and had been to Nicaragua a bunch of times, so I followed him out . . . into the deserted parking lot . . . in almost total darkness. Unfazed, Jeff stepped on the rear bumper of the pickup and pulled himself up and over the tailgate into the open truck bed. I proceeded likewise. We stood in the front of the black plastic-lined bed and grabbed onto the roll bar. Jimmy pulled back onto the road, and off we went. Okay, *this* was different. Now that we were out of the city, less subject to wrongdoers, and traveling more slowly, Jeff and I would complete the drive alfresco. The differences from my day-to-day routine were starting to pile up.

The paved, well-lit, two-lane thoroughfares of the city had yielded to semimaintained one-lane roads, and soon—as we began climbing from sea level to one thousand feet—to narrow, rutted dirt paths. I realized why our truck bore little resemblance to the pickups I see in my suburban neighborhoods at home. The large tires and reinforced suspension handled the uneven terrain with ease, and Jimmy managed the manual transmission like a pro, minimizing intergear lurches over the frequent and dramatic incline changes. Jeff assured me that this was the only road to and from the compound and that Jimmy drove it regularly.

This brotherly input was one of countless pieces of insight Jeff gave me prior to and during the trip. I have seen him grow over the years in this regard; he used to favor a more condescending tone when relating his life experiences or giving advice. Now he is more often unassuming, suggesting things to do or ways to act rather than delegating and directing. He and I agree that the deepening of his faith, coupled with the typical mellowing that comes with age, has improved his character in this regard.

Returning to the steep, winding ascent to Pochocuape, I looked to Jeff's steady demeanor—much like I focus on a flight attendant's calm temperament during air turbulence—to remain *tranquilo*. After about ten minutes, Jimmy turned right, into a short stone-covered driveway and stopped before a solid steel gate, some twenty feet wide and ten to twelve feet high, with the words *"Embajada del Cielo"* (Embassy of Heaven) and "Samaritans International" painted in large white letters. Below the letters were an array of tiny handprints in bright primary colors. My eyes trained on the barbed wire across the top and the guard tower to the right, rising above the adjacent concrete wall—stark contrasts to the childhood images below. A few blasts of the truck's horn and the gate creaked open, and in we pulled, coming to a stop in a dirt clearing between blue and orange pastel-painted concrete buildings. The heavy steel door clanged shut behind us, a night-piercing starter's pistol for my mission.

3

Secretly Incredible

We climbed out of the truck bed and were greeted by a friendly looking, middle-aged, light-skinned man in a purple polo with sweat stains around the armpits and midsection. He was full-bodied and bald and sported a thin grayish-brown goatee. As his hand extended for mine, I was surprised to hear him say in a sharp North Carolina twang, "Howdy, Bill! It's mighty nice ta meetcha!" This was Patrick Brown, Dedrick's brother, who ran Samaritans International of Nicaragua. He was the man in charge. *El Jefe.*

Since childhood, Patrick's life had prepared him for his present role. When he was ten years old, his father took him to a Christian revival concert, and a year later, they went to Brazil to visit a Christian ministry. His church upbringing involved a number of different denominations and faith practices, paving the way for his current ministry in the ecumenical environment of Nicaragua. Patrick attended a Bible college and was on track to become a pastor, at one point in his twenties living out of a motorhome and traveling to various communities up and down the East Coast to preach and spread the Gospel. The nomadic lifestyle prepared him for the transient life of a missionary.

Patrick's faith journey took a big turn—actually, it came to a screeching halt—in his late twenties when he ruptured his appendix, experienced grave infection, and became temporarily addicted to painkillers. "I was done serving God. I joined the business world and had dreams of being a millionaire in my thirties. For six years, I did not walk with the Lord." Like his prior life experiences, his time in business prepared him for his present responsibilities—in this case, in the areas of management, finance and accounting, and supply chain. Perhaps God's hand was at work preparing him for the future.

In Patrick's mid-thirties, an employee came into his store late one night, laid a gun on the counter, and said that Patrick had thirty minutes to convince the employee why he should not kill himself. Not knowing what to do, Patrick rummaged through a desk drawer and pulled out a Bible and started reading various passages. After a long conversation, including a speakerphone conversation with Patrick's father, the man accepted Jesus into his life and left without further incident. Patrick noted how "God is God, whether we want to admit it or not. God used me that night even though I wasn't walking with Jesus."

A few months after that fateful night—when Patrick still "remained apart from the Lord"—his father invited him on a mission trip to Guyana with twenty-eight pastors to preach to local Guyanese who traced their roots to India. Patrick saw his role as logistics and project management, not ministry. He described how, at one point, the pastors and a great crowd of Indians were on their knees praying, and all of a sudden, the entire group bent facedown to the ground and prayed for Patrick to reaccept Jesus into his life.

"There we were, in the middle of the jungle, and all these locals were praying for *me*! I mean, wow! I experienced God on that trip like I never had before." Patrick would never turn away from his faith again.

Fast-forwarding a few years, Patrick and his wife sold everything they owned and, with an infant daughter, moved to Peru to establish a feeding center in an impoverished community. Less than two months into their stay, Patrick placed a routine call to his dad, who had by then started Samaritans International of Nicaragua. His father was crying, saying he was going to have to close the Nicaraguan operation because some of his employees and suppliers had been stealing from him and because he was out of money. He asked Patrick if he could board a plane *that day* and relocate to Managua; maybe together, they could somehow fix things.

Only six weeks into their Peru commitment, Patrick and his wife all of a sudden had a huge decision to make. While they did not leave that day, they did fly to Nicaragua two days later. That flight was nine years prior to me climbing out of that pickup truck and shaking Patrick's hand for the first time. His marriage did not survive the time in Nicaragua, but Patrick turned around the operation, drawing on his long history of preparatory life experiences, starting with that first revival concert over three decades earlier.

As we said hello, others gathered behind Patrick, including a few of the American adults and teenagers who had arrived earlier on my intended flight from Miami. The faces were new, but a few of the voices were familiar from pretrip orientation calls. After handshakes all around, accompanied by what seemed like an inordinate—and warming—amount of eye contact and smiles, I felt instantly welcomed into this strange group in this strange place. The scene was now set for an unparalleled physical, mental, emotional, and spiritual experience, like being on a roller coaster just completing its initial clack-clack-clack ascent, ready to rocket into the twists and turns ahead.

After a long day of travel and so many new, amiable faces, I was struck by the notion of humility—in this case, how small my place was in the world—and how little I knew about people and what motivates them. Here was this group of teenagers who had decided to spend a week in a country with virtually none of the technology, media, or domestic comforts to which we North Americans are accustomed. Most had little idea what they had signed up for, yet something compelled each on this six-day sojourn rather than on the Caribbean travel option, which entailed some manual labor but also beach time, ocean swims, and resort living, or a domestic Habitat for Humanity gig with US hotel accommodations and video gaming consoles at their disposal. While there was a Facebook page for parents and friends to follow the Nicaragua J-term trip, none of these kids was there for self-promoting social media glory. This was down-and-dirty ministry—hard days' work for (only) hard days' spiritual pay.

Reflecting on the selflessness of these kids makes me think of the book *Love Does*, Bob Goff's entertaining and impactful autobiographical compilation of life lessons. Goff says God wants us to be "secretly incredible" rather than wear a cape like a superhero. "It's like [Jesus] was saying what if we were just to do awesome, incredible stuff together while we're here on earth, and only He knew would be enough?" And I had not yet begun to appreciate the locals' humble approach to their duties, which I would learn personified what the Bible says in 1 Peter 5:5: "Clothe yourselves with humility in your dealings with one another, for 'God opposes the proud but bestows favor on the humble.'"

Humility is becoming less important in the developed—privileged—world. As a boy in the 1980s, I recall seeing "I love NY" logos all over Manhattan, conveying the idea that individuals could connect themselves to a ginormous, dynamic place like New York City. It was understood and accepted that the wearer of a T-shirt or drinker from a coffee mug with the slogan on it was minuscule compared to the Big Apple; people knew their relative place and significance. It was humbling. Fast-forwarding to recent years, I have been struck by how these well-known and seemingly timeless tourist tchotchkes now share the coveted sidewalk displays along the avenues and cross streets with "NY loves Me" shirts and knickknacks, conjured in the same format as their polar predecessors. Emblematic of the everyone-gets-a-trophy trend in American society, the perceived priority has flipped from the greater good to the individual. It seems that, in much of North America—and likely elsewhere—as we watch humility wane, we see narcissism wax.

Pride is narcissism's genteel, covert cousin, what C. S. Lewis calls "the great sin" and "a spiritual cancer: It eats up the very possibility of love or contentment or even common sense." No form of religion or spiritual ethos I have studied condones an attitudinal ordering that puts self above others. John Eldredge's *Beautiful Outlaw*, a scrappy, plain-speak biography of Jesus Christ, speaks to pride as well, relating the story early in His earthly ministry when Jesus arrives at the River Jordan while John the Baptist was baptizing hordes of people: "Jesus files down bankside with the rest of the crowd. . . . Nobody gives him a second glance. He's just another sunbaked Jew in robe and sandals, taking his turn like a guy at a deli waiting for his number to be called."

First integrity and now humility. I had been in Nicaragua less than two hours and could already sense how the character whetstone might hone me in the days to come.

4

Domestic Contrasts

arrived at the compound after everyone had eaten dinner, but the staff had prepared a plate for me. Before starting my meal, Jeff directed me to a small shallow basin on a table by the food. He said it contained bleach water and I should dip my hands in it, wipe them with a paper towel, and then use hand sanitizer (the mission was prepandemic, so such practices were not as ubiquitous). We were sternly instructed in pretrip communications and during the week not to drink the tap water—or to ingest any in the shower or nick ourselves shaving—because our bodies lacked the proper enzymes to process the local bacteria. While, in one sense, being at risk from drinking the water was not a big deal (I had had Montezuma's revenge as a child during a Caribbean family vacation), in another sense, it was quite symbolic: For one of the few times in my life, I was the foreigner, a member of the minority, of the disadvantaged group.

Exacerbating this compromised position was the omnipresence of one of the most telltale symbols of American travel, the

16.9-ounce (500-milliliter) plastic water bottle. We would consume crazy amounts of them on the trip, staying hydrated in the heat and humidity but producing huge amounts of waste in a country ill-equipped to recycle it. And we chaperones would regularly have to remind the kids not to leave half-full bottles lying around. I have heard that our trip was one of the last not to employ reusable bottles and large, portable water tanks, so thankfully, the prevalence of this ugly American symbol has diminished.

My initial experience with water led to a series of other creature comfort and take-for-granted differences in Central America. For context, *Embajada del Cielo* was designed to house American missionaries, so our rooms' appointments—while basic by our standards—were far superior to the homes in the surrounding community and across much of the country. With that said, each bathroom's hot water was supplied by what the veteran missionaries called a "widowmaker." The device was installed next to the shower head and heated the water as it passed to the spigot. The person showering would turn on the electric heating element by hand while standing in the running shower. Electricity. Turning a metal knob. Standing in water. You get the idea. The quality and grounding of the wiring were unknown, with no visible certification stamps like you would see in the States from the National Electrical Code or OSHA.

The sleeping conditions were spartan, a hodgepodge of beds and mattresses covered with sheets and blankets of random colors and patterns. My bed was topped with a gray, faded airline blanket. Anyone who has flown knows how flimsy these coverings are, and mine was dated; it bore the US Air logo, a name not in use since the 1990s. The blanket quality mattered because—again acknowledging our privilege relative to the locals—we had air conditioning, and one of my roommates insisted on keeping the thermostat set to arctic. My undersized covering provided little warmth for my tall frame.

For the furniture, recall that the Brown family owns a stateside furniture store, so while few of the beds, hutches, and tables matched, most were of good quality, having been shipped down in the forty-foot-long international shipping containers that transported SWH's food to Nicaragua.

The starkest of domestic contrasts involved the toilets. This difference was weird, and I apologize in advance. While the toilets were similar to the ones at home and did flush, the plumbing system could handle only human waste, not paper products. So you had to, ahem, wipe yourself with toilet paper and then sort of pile the used pieces next to the john. Once finished, you carried the paper to an outside trash can. I found this to be the compound's most comfort-zone-abandoning feature. It was admittedly minor in the scheme of things but new to me just the same, another (small) opportunity to build character.

A major irony of our mission involved the meals we ate. Servants With a Heart's core purpose is to provide food to underserved communities; lack of quality food is literally why we were there. But we Americans—*los gringos,* as some affectionately called us—ate well; my evening meal that first night consisted of baked chicken leg and thigh, white rice, and green beans. Our food was well balanced and well prepared, our Samaritans hosts thoughtfully and dutifully cooking meals to power us through our days and keeping our ill-prepared bodies functioning. I reflect how, through my "normal" lens, I might view such fare as bland and mundane, but this new perspective revealed that our options were royal compared to what filled the table of most locals. Privilege, again poking out its head.

On a much lighter note, one of the other chaperones was Jeff's close friend, Charles Roebuck, president of his family's fourth-generation printing business in Baltimore. Jeff and Charles had become fast friends in college, were in each other's weddings, and have remained tight throughout adulthood. Charles—sometimes Chuck in our family—is one of the most affable, humble people I know. His kindness is unsurpassed. I love his keen wit, steady stream of self-deprecating jokes, and ability to quote an inordinate amount of movie lines (a "talent" we share). Reflecting on the quality of the food from the prior year's J-term (his first mission), Charles smirked that only he could have managed to *gain* weight on a food ministry trip.

After my quick dinner for one (as the youngest of five, I am—for better and worse—a fast eater), Jeff gave me an orientation of the compound. The barbed-wire-capped perimeter walls encircled an upper and lower section of buildings, separated by a subtle incline with a low-rise set of concrete steps . . . the kind on which you are never sure whether to take one stride per step or two. Having had four ACL surgeries on my left knee, I usually opted for two. The upper level consisted of the kitchen and dining area, where we met as a group and took our meals; the Samaritans International offices (one of only two two-story buildings at the *Embajada*); a schoolhouse consisting of a half dozen classrooms oriented in a straight line; and a longer blue, yellow, and green building with additional offices and classrooms. These buildings—like all those in the compound—were constructed of concrete with corrugated aluminum roofs . . . simple yet durable and insulated from the heat, as not all buildings had air conditioning.

At the far end of this level stood the chapel, which resembled most churches in Nicaragua: simple, square structures with walls of cinder block or industrial siding, roofs of aluminum or plywood, and dirt floors; the nicer ones *might* have electricity. I compared these settings to the houses of worship I knew from home—mostly majestic gothic or Georgian edifices with soaring bell towers, ornate stained-glass windows, deeply varnished mahogany pews, and elaborate, elevated marble altars.

Surpassing these contrasts in finish and formality, however, is that "church" in rural Nicaragua, as in much of the developing world, relates more to the term's original—and I would argue more important—biblical description: "Built on the foundation of the apostles and prophets, with Christ Jesus himself as the capstone. Through him the whole structure is held together and grows into a temple sacred in the Lord" (Ephesians 2:20–21). Places of worship are about common faith, about believers and morals, not bricks and mortar.

The lower, rearward section of the compound consisted mostly of sleeping quarters—a series of rooms oriented in two rows facing each other, reminiscent of an interstate motel. This dormitory area was on a gradual downslope, the ground consisting of hard-packed clay backboned by a concrete, semicircular rain gutter about five feet across that channeled rainy-season deluges. At the downhill end of these quarters were the warehouse, where the mission food was stored, and the two-story home where Patrick's family lived. Painted in giant white block letters on the wall of the home was the apostle Paul's famous passage from 1 Corinthians: "Faith, hope, and love. The greatest of these is love," the word *LOVE* done in capital letters.

Beyond the warehouse was another gate, opening to a working hilltop farm where Patrick's daughter cultivated various indigenous vegetables, fruits, and herbs and tended to egg-laying chickens and milk-producing goats. I learned a sobering factoid about the farm area: This hilltop was part of an evacuation plan if major political unrest or another emerging threat forced us to flee. Such contingency planning, like the presence of armed security liaisons, was far more about abundance of caution than likelihood of need.

The tour culminated with a stop by our dorm room, which I would be sharing with Jeff and Charles. Everyone then gathered in the dining area—my first chance to absorb the entirety of the group. In the room were the fourteen high schoolers and us five

American chaperones, along with about a half dozen members of the Samaritans staff, including Patrick and Jimmy and a few others I would get to know as the week unfolded.

All the Americans wore matching T-shirts, a unique and simplifying custom of mission trips. You may have noticed groups of people in airports clad in coordinating, brightly colored shirts, often with a cross or country map on one side and perhaps a Bible verse on the other. Ours sported the Servants With a Heart logo large on the back, small on the left breast: two lithe hands holding a heart-shaped earth, all circled by the foundation's name and the motto "Serving Families Worldwide." The matching shirts promote the mission, provide a convenient way to count your ducklings, and simplify packing requirements. Win–win–win.

5

So You Went on a Mission Trip?

While Jeff and Suzanne's seeds of connection to Nicaragua were sown at that aforementioned lunch with Dedrick and Nancy Brown, the green shoots of the J-term trip were cultivated with Rone (pronounced like "lone") and his wife, January. The two couples had gotten acquainted through a food-packing event and through Charlotte Christian, where both families attended. The Yohs and Reeds had also been on mission trips to Managua, although not together. Then, at a back-to-school night at which the principal talked about J-term, Rone mentioned in passing that the Yohs should start a Nicaragua trip for the students to distribute their food. As Rone described it, "In typical Jeff fashion, he immediately said, 'Great idea—as long as you run it with us.'"

The early J-term trips—which Rone likes to call *Jesus terms* instead of *January terms*—were a combination of VBS (vacation Bible school) and food distribution. The two couples shared planning and implementation tasks seamlessly, forming what Rone called "a great leadership story of selfless servants operating as one body." After a few years, they phased out VBS, believing that the food ministry afforded deeper immersion and relationship building.

When not running high school mission trips or otherwise being active in his communities, Rone is a husband and father of two, both of whom were on our trip, and works in wealth management, leading a team of professionals supporting high-net-worth families. A West Point graduate, Rone's distinguished military career culminated as a Special Forces A-Team commander. While he was not able to tell me much about what he did on active duty, I gleaned enough to know he spent *a lot* of time on foreign soil—and that our nation is the safer for it. Thank you, former Team Commander Reed.

In the dining area that night, Rone introduced me to the group with a thinly veiled barb toward his good friend and fellow Charlotte resident, Jeff, saying something like "This is Bill, Jeff's younger, smarter, better-looking brother." True or not, I had just met this Green Beret so didn't risk correcting him!

Rone then explained an important exercise we would do each night that underscored a goal for the week: While our mission was to minister to locals with food, games, and the Word of God, the time was also designed to benefit us North Americans. At the heart of what Jeff and Rone and Patrick hoped to promote was relationship building, with both Nicaraguans and fellow missionaries, perhaps to discover new and authentic ways to experience love for God and for each other. Over the years, Jeff and Suzanne, aided by Rone and other past chaperones, had developed the exercise called "Telling Your Story" into a series of daily reflections intended to increase the missionaries' awareness of the trip's impact. Rone explained how the exercise was also designed to help answer the question each of us would surely receive when we got home: "So, you went on a mission trip. How was it?"

We were each given a two-page handout with instructions, blank fields, and empty tables. Each night, our team would gather—boys with the men, girls with the women—to debrief the day; meeting by gender was intended to encourage candor. The first part of each gathering would be silent time to reflect on and capture the day's highlights. We would then take turns sharing our musings and discussing the similarities and differences among our observations.

As the week unfolded, these evening reflections proved to be almost as impactful as the events that inspired them. I called the male students "boys" above, but their—and the girls'—ability to digest, interpret, and express what they experienced each day was as mature as any grownup might convey. Later in the week, each person would distill their daily takeaways into meta-observations, as well as conclusions about what God had put on their heart and, finally, the words for answering the "how was your trip" query.

What a life skill. How often do we take the time to reflect on what we do? Life seems to get busier and busier, with technology's flywheel productivity enhancements and society and social media's ever-increasing expectations of achievement and personal brand, all occurring at breakneck pace. Knowing we would spend time each night contemplating our shared experiences was sure to build bonds and deepen the experience for all. Kudos to the group leaders who imparted to these young people such a universally applicable and life-enhancing practice.

Reflection and introspection are hard work, which is the final facet of character I observed from the first day of the mission. Who among us is inclined to look in the mirror regularly and assess what we have done—and what we have left undone? It is difficult to do. My parents always worked hard, my dad running the family business, my mom running our household of seven, and both of them actively participating in and leading various charitable and community organizations. My four older siblings have always worked hard as well. My wife, Kelly, might be the hardest-working person I know. Whether it was excelling in graduate school, teaching full-time, raising our children, or now running the small business we own, caring for older relatives, and teaching part-time, she is the ultimate manifestation of a strong work ethic.

I have always been surrounded by hardworking people, and I would like to think it has rubbed off. I was a strong student in school, excelled in sports, held leadership positions in high school and college, and then spent almost twenty-five years full-time in the business world, (hopefully) demonstrating a strong work ethic for others to emulate. More recently, as my writing, academic, and volunteer efforts have filled much of my previous corporate bandwidth, I have tried to continue to apply myself with rigor in whatever I do, modeling for my three children what hard work looks like. Our culture seems to blur the lines between true hard work and hollow-calorie busyness; distinguishing that wheat from that chaff attaches intentionality and purpose to the important—and hard—things we do.

While I had only been in Nicaragua a few hours, it was already apparent that the Samaritans staffers I had met also personified hard work, likely beyond my own experiences. Jimmy's journey from refugee to mission leader, Patrick's decision to give up the relative comforts of North Carolina for his faith calling thousands of miles from home, and the compound's kitchen and maintenance staff, whose toil was apparent in the quality of the food and level of upkeep of the accommodations. And as the coming days unfolded, I would witness even greater expressions of industry, particularly backdropped by Nicaragua's lack of the technology and capital investment that facilitate so much of the life I knew in the States.

The New Testament says, "In every way I have shown you that by hard work of that sort we must help the weak, and keep in mind the words of the Lord Jesus who himself said, 'It is more blessed to give than to receive'" (Acts 20:35). In *The Road to Character*, author David Brooks writes how developing character can be a grind. "Character is not innate or automatic. You have to build it with effort and artistry." In a simple yet profound comparison of what he calls "résumé virtues" versus "eulogy virtues," Brooks contends that "most of us have clearer strategies for how to achieve career success than we do for how to develop a profound character."

David Livermore, author of *Serving with Eyes Wide Open*, a reflection on and primer for short-term mission trips that I read the month before, discusses the toil of building deep relationships. "To love people is to get involved in their lives. That's messy and complicated"—two apt words to describe what some of the coming days would bring.

When our evening meetings concluded, curfew was set for the kids (not like they had any way of breaching the concrete walls and barbed wire—nor would they want to, given the lack of proximate teenage attractions), and we retired to our rooms. After washing up with bottled water, I chatted with Jeff and Charles, noting how weird it was to have woken up in Pennsylvania with Kelly that morning and to be going to sleep in Nicaragua with them that night. Both of them (veteran J-termers) recalled their first impressions from prior trips, the ease of their rapport reminding me how deep and special their relationship was.

Sleeping in a strange place and chatting with my brother and his good friend took me back in time, first to dormitory living in college, then to high school weekends at friends' houses, and eventually to childhood sleepaway camp. There is something unique, almost primal, about the final conversation you have before falling asleep and about the last person with whom you have it. The experience is personal, revealing, intimate—that brief spell when your brain begins filing the day's thoughts and events.

As I drifted off below my vintage (and not in a good way) airline blanket, I was aware of the choices we had each made: Jeff to invite me, to invite Charles, to initiate J-term in Nicaragua, to create Servants With a Heart with Suzanne, and on and on; Charles—who admits to being not the most religious person in the world—to accept Jeff's invitation, stretching beyond his or most people's comfort zone, and to return for a second year; and me, to also accept Jeff's offer, leaving my family at the end of winter break, knowing little about the place and experience into which I had plunged.

Reflecting on all these decisions reminds me how a few of my friends refer to Christianity as a contact sport; you have to engage with others—be in relationship—for it to matter. Hinduism espouses a similar philosophy, as described in *An Introduction to Hinduism* by the scholar Gavin Flood, who says a key characteristic of this Eastern religion is that "practice takes precedent over belief. What a Hindu does is more important than what a Hindu believes." Engagement and relationship are choices we make, choices that both build and reveal our character.

That first night, I realized my choice to go on this trip was not something random or something I conjured internally. In fact, I didn't even initiate it. I was there because God, coursing through me as the Holy Spirit, had led me to Pochocuape.

Part 2

MONDAY: DIGNITY

If love is connection, then the experience of having our dignity honored is what creates the connection.

—DONNA HICKS, *Leading with Dignity*

6

Uppercut of Reality

I don't consider myself a country boy or a city boy, more of a suburbs boy. I have lived briefly in Madrid, San Francisco, and Philadelphia, but since the late '90s, I have been in the western suburbs of Philadelphia. So when the first thing I heard Monday morning in Nicaragua was a rooster's crow, it was an instant reminder I was somewhere different. I wondered how to say "cock-a-doodle-do" in Spanish?

After donning shorts and the day's prescribed red Servants With a Heart T-shirt, I made my way to the dining area, where fresh-brewed coffee awaited. I love coffee and often grind Central American beans at home. Presuming these beans were grown somewhere nearby made my morning joe all the more enjoyable. As adults and children trickled in, I observed varied circadian rhythms at work: Some people bounded into the room, their I'm-a-morning-person-and-isn't-life-great energy bringing the maroon cinder block walls to life. I'm part of this group, often at home evoking grunts and harrumphs from my wife and kids. Others in the group shuffled in, eyes to the floor, bedhead dos and mopey expressions signaling physical presence but a mental inability to absorb information just yet. We prayed as a group and then ate, the women and girls getting their food before the men and boys. The food did what food does, providing requisite calories for the day and also creating a bond and closeness among us, the long cafeteria-style picnic tables facilitating eye contact and conversation.

After breakfast, we performed our first mission task—packing small toy bags for the children we would see later. We covered the rows of tables with piles of small figurines, games, and assorted knickknacks and filled small pink bags for girls and small blue bags for boys with gender-intended playthings. Following the ladies-first food service, I thought about how interesting—and arbitrary—the world can be. I don't mean this as altogether negative; I believe living in a civilized society requires customs and rituals, part of both the glue and the lubricant that allow people to live in harmony. More specifically, I believe it is important to acknowledge gender differentiation and how God intended each of us through creation and at conception.

But society—especially in the States—is changing. Similar to the contrast in perceptions about locally sourced food on my drive from the airport the night before, I compare the toy packing's traditional pink-and-blue color designations to an observation from back home. There is a birthing center around the corner from me in Pennsylvania, where some women elect to have their babies, aided by midwives committed to providing a more holistic and natural environment than a maternity ward might. The center is across the street from a major hospital—I assume for access to more acute care should the need arise. Each time a baby is born at the birthing center, the workers hang a small flag out the window proclaiming "It's a boy!" or "It's a girl!" For many years, the flags were blue and pink, respectively, and there would typically be several blowing in the wind by nightfall, providing a what-really-matters reminder on my early evening commute.

Over the past few years, however, the flags have changed to various and random colors, no longer adhering to the traditional blue-for-boys and pink-for-girls practice. I am okay with this palette proliferation given the many, often invisible ways we inadvertently disempower girls or unnecessarily emphasize the relevance of gender and male privilege. Recently, however, I have wondered how the birthing center flags would adapt should certain patients elect not to assign a sex to their newborns. As for me, I believe "It's a boy!" and "It's a girl!" are reflections of biological fact.

I also believe that we should recognize the dignity inherent in each of us. Every person is unique, has innate value, and possesses the right to live a life of meaning. Whether male or female, straight or gay, white or black or brown, young or old, rich or poor, someone we consider a friend or someone who might be at odds with our worldview, I believe that the most *human* thing we can do and the most *humane* thing we can do is acknowledge the dignity in every person, regardless of how similar or different we may be.

I have become keenly attuned to tensions of similarity and difference as I reflect on my life. I was born white. I was born male. I was born in the United States. I was born without any physical or mental impairments. And I was born to married parents and grew up in an affluent neighborhood. I received a top-notch education. Today, I am middle-aged, I am married with children, we live comfortably, and we practice Christianity. I am tall, and I am heterosexual. From just about every angle, my position in life has given me advantages, given me the lightning-rod concept of privilege. There is an expression that says, "You see that guy over there? He was born on third base but thinks he hit a triple." As a die-hard sports fan, I appreciate the analogy. As a born-on-third guy, I know I did not get there on my own.

So I did not come to Nicaragua to save the world or with any notion that the ministry I would provide would sustainably move the needle for anyone I encountered. While I was not familiar then with the term *white savior complex*, I do not believe I or any of us came with any such presupposition about our role or influence. But I did come to push myself, to do what I could, at the heartfelt suggestion of my brother, to connect with other human beings—perhaps to experience a new and deeper form of relationship and love—in hopes of doing what God would like me to do. Our work that week would accelerate my awareness of base path positioning and privilege.

After filling the toy sacks, we went to our rooms to pack day bags, swap out flip-flops for trail shoes and sneakers, and apply sunblock. We then gathered in our red T-shirts to take our first daily group photo, which would be uploaded to the trip's Facebook page, an efficient way to mollify stateside relatives anxious about the students' well-being. On a previous J-term trip, the morning snapshot had been given a clear but macabre title: the proof-of-life photo. The feedback was that parents appreciated the dark humor, so the name stuck.

We loaded into a large cage truck, its bars along the sides and back of the bed. The students sat in the front of the flatbed and used boxes of food as seats. The other chaperones and I stood behind them, using the metal bars for stability. In the far back were our purple-shirted Samaritans guides, interpreters, and security guards, with whom we would interact more and more as the week evolved. We departed the compound for the Mateare trash dump. As daunting as the prior evening's journey up the hill to Pochocuape had been, the trip down that morning was differently dicey. Rather than traveling in the tough Hilux, made for rutty climbs, we were now in a gigantic flatbed truck, tough in its own right but, in my mind, not designed for steep descents on uneven, unpaved trails.

The truck did fine, although there was one particularly sharp bend in the trail where the roadside dropped off several feet on one side, the truck's large tires coming close to the unreinforced edge. I have a fear of heights and recall the quick but sinking feeling in my midsection as we benignly rolled past the drop-off. I had to bob and weave a few times along the drive to avoid tree branches hanging in our path. The foliage triggered my first real chaperone duty, calling out "Tree!" and "Duck!" to alert the chatty students—riding with typical and endearing adolescent oblivion—to protect themselves as branches and fronds whipped over and along the cage.

Mateare is among the most dire of the eight-hundred-plus feeding sites Samaritans International supports across Nicaragua. As Patrick later related in his sharp North Carolina accent, seemingly unmellowed after eight years living abroad, "No one comes here. No one helps these people. No one cares about these people. And so we come, and we feed them, and we bring medicines. We show them the love of Christ. And y'all being here is a huge blessing to them. They count it as an honor just for you to walk into their life, because this is not just a couple hours of time to them. They live here and work here all week, every week. They're out here in the sun and in the smoke. They're out here in the rainy season. It doesn't matter."

Patrick's remarks underscore a critical dynamic of mission work. Samaritans first gained access to Mateare—and to many other destitute communities—through offers of food and medicine, lifesaving provisions. They did not lead with Christ and the offer to bring the Good News of the Gospel. They have learned that while some groups are open to and excited about "the whole Jesus thing," others are understandably more motivated by access to food, which is lacking in so many places.

This interplay between the food and the Word is fascinating. Jesus said, "I am the bread of life; whoever comes to me will never hunger" (John 6:35). His earthly ministry followed a pattern of first addressing underserved people's needs and then providing the "why" of God and faith and salvation. Both in the Gospels and on our mission, the bread of life and the cup of salvation are shared, and both are consumed. The art of the mission is determining with which to lead.

The conditions at Mateare, which I described in the beginning of the book, were like nothing I had ever experienced. I had never envisioned what visiting—let alone living in—a trash dump would be like.

Rone, our mission team leader, explained why we started our week as we did: "I took the group there first by design. I wanted to give them an uppercut of reality, to shake them to their core. I wanted everyone to rethink their life and what happiness means at the beginning of the trip. If we can crack that shell early on, the soil is more fertile for the subsequent activities that lead to an evolution in faith. The seeds of faith find the fertile ground and accelerate growth, in both the kids and in the adults."

Rone's intentionality illustrates a valuable and not necessarily intuitive dynamic of mission work: Who were we helping, the Nicaraguans or ourselves? Who was ministering to whom? It is pretty obvious that providing food to hungry people helps them. But it was not clear to me then how our efforts might circle back, how we privileged North Americans would be nourished as well. The profundity of Rone's words would come up again and again as the week unfolded.

I have now been on three overseas mission trips in the past few years. On each trip, our group was reminded of mission trip expert David Livermore's direction not to "pet the poor." We were prepared by stories of locals' reactions to American perceptions of their situations, the locals expressing sentiments like "Gee, that's funny. I didn't realize I was poor until you [Americans] told me I was." No one on these trips was impressed by where we lived or where we went to school or what version iPhone we had. The materialism and social (media) status of our lives did not matter. The number of zeros in our bank accounts did not register to those whose bank accounts were zero.

I discovered, as did our students—what a gift at their ages—that flaunting any American one-upmanship was pointless and self-incriminating. On these trips, I have interacted with hundreds of Central Americans and Africans, people with whom I have virtually no commonality on paper. But through conversations and shared experiences, I discovered that many of us held a common faith, a common belief that there exists something greater than us, a common understanding that there is a hand at the tiller of our lives influencing the rudder and therefore the direction of our temporal voyages.

Through the lens of dignity, I appreciated this common ground. Matthew's Gospel quotes Jesus as saying, "Whatever you did for one of the least of these brothers and sisters of mine, you did for me" (Matthew 25:40, NIV). But even this text, one of the most referenced of Jesus's numerous teachings, could yield a modern-day impression of hierarchy—an I-am-more-than-these-"least"-people dynamic—that belies dignity's inherent equality. I have realized through these trips how much privilege I have . . . and how utterly meaningless it can be.

At home I participate in a Thursday morning Gospel reflection at my parish, where a collection of men gather to read the coming Sunday's scripture passages and discuss how they apply to our lives. One of the participants has ALS—Lou Gehrig's disease—a terminal affliction that erodes the nervous system such that all of the sufferer's muscles eventually stop working. Its cause is unknown, and there is no cure. ALS has claimed my aunt, my neighbor, and two of my childhood friends, and now it has gripped a fellow parishioner. It is awful. At the beginning of each session, the group takes turns reading a few prayers aloud to set the tone. My friend's ALS has taken his speech, so each time it is his turn to read, the group remains silent for the approximate time it would take to recite that passage. This small but considerate act connects us and provides the pinnacle of dignity in my weekly routine.

New York Times best-selling author James Redfield writes in *The Celestine Prophecy* about the connectedness among people, referring to the importance of "learning to perceive what was formerly an invisible type of energy . . . an energy field hovering about everything." He contends that as people focus more of their attention on each other, an actual force emerges between them, a force that can both pinpoint one's perception due to its focus and blur one's vision due to its power. The medical field may say these sensory changes are triggered by oxytocin—the "love hormone."

Either way, I experienced this phenomenon once in the mid-1990s (not surprisingly shortly after reading *The Celestine Prophecy*) with my future wife, Kelly. Sitting on a futon one afternoon in my flat in San Francisco, where I lived in my twenties, she and I were looking at each other when the outline of her face started to blur. I recall feeling a strange yet invigorating pulse rise through me. My eyes were not watering, but her image became fuzzy (and no, there had been no sensory-altering day drinking). I had this euphoric sense of connectedness I had never felt before. At that moment, only a few months after we had met, I first told Kelly I loved her. Our connectedness—the energy between us and the dignity I felt for her—was palpable.

Secular lenses see the importance of dignity and human connection as well. Dale Carnegie, in his seminal 1930s tome *How to*

Win Friends and Influence People, relates how a business interaction showed him the importance of honoring others:

> Oh yes, I did want something out of that chap. I wanted something priceless. And I got it. I got the feeling that I had done something for him without his being able to do anything whatever in return for me. . . . Almost all the people you meet feel themselves superior to you in some way, and a sure way to their hearts is to let them realize in some subtle way that you recognize their importance, and recognize it sincerely.

Carnegie's commentary underscores the notions of mutual benefit and who is ministering to whom. A Canadian scientist coined the phrase *altruistic egoism* to describe how the act of helping someone else is also helping yourself, that thinking and acting on behalf of others can make us feel good internally—a justifiable selfishness. It seems focusing on relationships, be it on a futon in San Francisco or in a Nicaraguan trash dump, is a win–win endeavor.

7

Female Faithful

When María, who you met in the prologue, said, "*Yo estoy contenta*" (I am happy), I and every other Servants With a Heart traveler were floored. My life lens had me wondering how she could feel happy . . . or any positive emotion? María had few possessions, presumably no steady income, and—particularly—no food for her family. Providing for one's children may be the most fundamental and primordial function a parent has, our ultimate *raison d'être*. But far too frequently, millions of mothers (and fathers) worldwide are food insecure.

According to The Hunger Project, over eight hundred million people in the world are chronically undernourished, 99 percent of whom live in developing countries (like Nicaragua), and nearly half of all deaths in children under five—accounting for three million dead annually—are attributed to undernutrition. Another fact David Livermore provides in *Serving with Eyes Wide Open* is that we Americans account for just 5 percent of the world's population but consume *50 percent* of the world's resources. I shudder at this statistic, thinking about the quantity of food, some expired, my family has in our refrigerators, freezers, and cupboards (note that all three are plural).

Livermore states that the problem with hunger across the globe is not humanity's ability to produce enough food but its inequitable distribution, plunging billions into starvation. Even the US is subject to chronic hunger. According to Feeding America—the nation's largest food bank—in 2018, almost forty million Americans were food insecure, and the recent pandemic has only increased this population. Exacerbating food insecurity and distribution issues is the increasing global wealth gap. Robin DiAngelo relates in *White Fragility* that, since 2015, the richest 1 percent of the world has owned more wealth than the rest of the planet combined, and between 1998 and 2011, that same 1 percent's income increased 182 times as fast as the earnings of the poorest 10 percent.

These statistics are scary—and motivating. Meeting María and hearing her story, however, made the epidemic of food insecurity *real*. Hunger and starvation were not just numbers in books and on websites but a reality right in front of me, smoldering all around me like the refuse I was standing in. But María didn't complain about her life; she expressed gratitude. When Patrick asked why she was happy, she responded (in Spanish, of course) that when she woke up that morning, she did not know how she was going to feed her family, so she prayed, and God sent us with the food, and that made her *contenta*. Of course she was probably not always happy. But in that moment, she showed a sincere way—a dignified way—to approach life, absent the trappings that cloud our North American am-I-happy-or-not barometers.

María was buoyed by her belief, what I call *unvarnished faith*: She prayed, and God answered. She did not question it, did not try to explain it some other way. Her worldview was not dressed up in doctrinal customs or shrouded in judgy platitudes. When you don't have a ton of things in your life to distort your priorities, you focus on the things that matter. In María's case, those things appeared to be caring for her family and having faith in God to provide for them. That's unvarnished faith at work.

I can't help but compare her attitude to how we act in many communities in the States. We have (relatively) everything we could need, but we are professional complainers. We gnash our teeth about anything and everything—slow Wi-Fi at Starbucks, oversalted sweet potato fries at Ruby Tuesdays, no open parking spots in front of the Apple Store. We are pros, rarely satisfied, always wanting what we don't have.

So many Americans choose to be unhappy and complain, not in spite of our materialism but in light of it. But María chose differently. Less than twenty-four hours before going to Mateare, I was on a layover in the Dallas/Fort Worth airport, sipping a Corona Lite and watching SportsCenter on three large flat-screen TVs. Now I was in a Central American waste site surrounded by burning refuse, hearing a soot-covered woman express gratitude for us stopping by. It might have been the most dignified thing I have ever experienced.

María's story speaks not just to the dignity of those in need but also to the dignity of women. For much of recorded time (dating back to when cave people scribbled on rock walls), women held a subordinate position to men, considered little more than property; patriarchal predominance reigned for thousands of years. Over the past half century or so, starting around the time of the invention of "the pill" in the 1960s, the role and rights of women in the developed world have advanced markedly, with women's liberation and gender equality groundswells permeating many facets of society. The past several decades have seen advances in education (today, more women than men attend college) and the professional world. One of my favorite television ads from the 2010s celebrated the expression *throw like a girl*, a clever and powerful inversion from the phrase's previous long-standing derogatory connotation.

However, responsibility discrepancies, glass ceilings, and pay gaps are still grim realities. There is a social media aphorism that helps describe the current situation: "We expect women to work like they don't have children and raise children like they don't work." Women of color have even more difficult obstacles to overcome. We need to eradicate these inequalities, leveling the playing field, the payroll ledger, and the boardroom table. And there remain far more unconscionable facets of gender inequality, namely the degradation, objectification, and persecution of women through human trafficking, prostitution, and pornography and the grotesque behavior of certain men, which led to the #MeToo movement.

Even world hunger is related to gender inequity. A former colleague of mine who left the corporate world to join The Hunger Project told me how the lack of women's rights and equality—key facets of dignity—is a major contributor to food insufficiency in much of the developing world. Compounding all of these forces are issues of gender identity and fluidity, which are now receiving more focus.

We still have much to do to achieve gender equality and dignity for women. As I reflect on these issues, however, I'm emboldened by my Christian faith. I am proud that during His ministry two millennia ago, Jesus was undoubtedly prowoman, in transformative and custom-shattering ways. Among the many revolutionary acts He performed and unprecedented ethos He espoused, His recognition of the dignity of women was among the greatest. As I stated above, at the time of Christ, women were considered little more than property, close to livestock. Marriage was a legal contract with no moral or religious covenant, and women possessed few rights. Their role was to procreate, to prepare food for and nurture their families, and generally to be seen and not heard.

Jesus's life, from beginning to end, belied these norms. When His mother, Mary, was pregnant with Him, she visited her cousin Elizabeth, who was pregnant with John the Baptist. Elizabeth's baby leaped in her womb when Mary and Jesus entered the room. This interaction, believed to indicate the presence of the Holy Spirit, involved two women and no adult men. Throughout Jesus's time on earth, there were myriad examples of equalizing and dignifying treatment of women. Two of my favorite include when the Syrophoenician woman showed Jesus something about ministry with the "table scraps for dogs" metaphor, and the parable of Mary and Martha, when Jesus asserted that women should be able to converse and interact with men as equals. And finally, at Jesus's resurrection—*the* most important moment in Christian history—it is notable (and was revolutionary) that He first revealed His resurrected self to women, appearing among them at the empty tomb. He could have chosen anyone, most obviously any of the eleven current disciples, but He chose women to unveil what Christians consider the greatest news ever.

Jesus's impact on our world is extraordinary. Time culturally restarted at His birth. From his initial dozen or so followers, more than two billion people now accept and practice His teachings. No two books have had a greater impact on Western civilization than the Old and New Testaments, and His life was the fusion between their initially disparate but profoundly connected messages. Jesus recognized and celebrated the dignity of women in groundbreaking fashion, doing so almost two thousand years ago. Society has taken a long, long time to catch up to and honor His example. We are not there yet. We must stay the course.

María was one of many women we encountered during our mission. The various churches and community centers we entered were populated mostly by women caring for children, guiding both their physical and spiritual nourishment. In addition to seeing women like María so committed to their families and their faith, I sensed something unique about how the female American chaperones and Samaritans International workers interacted with the local children. Their loving stares and warm hugs showed the universality of the maternal instinct, one of many examples from my six days in Pochocuape of how much people can communicate without saying a thing. Perhaps dignity expressed by action is more authentic than dignity expressed by words.

One of our Samaritans hosts was Jackie, a thirtyish Nicaraguan woman who attended the same church as Jimmy and had met Patrick through him. She had a degree in pharmacy but was drawn to a life of faith and mission work. After a few years volunteering, she became a full-time Samaritans employee two years before our trip. In addition to translating for the Americans, Jackie facilitated many of the missionaries' interactions in the communities. She had straight, dark brown hair, wore tortoiseshell eyeglasses, and carried herself with a natural bounce and lightness of foot that conveyed enthusiasm and forward motion. Her bubbly smile and friendly demeanor helped ease any tension or protective instincts village matriarchs might have had toward outsiders, empathizing with those town centurions and appreciating their dignity in ways male Samaritans employees—and all Americans—could not.

Jackie connected with the village children as well, enabled by her energy and relative youth. She told me a story from a few months earlier involving a boy who had been stealing food. No one was able to peg his motive—until Jackie: "This little boy, about ten or eleven years old, told me that he was stealing the food from the feeding center. He had never told anyone this. So I was like, 'Why do you do that? We try to provide enough food for everyone.' He said he had like seven or eight brothers and sisters, and in their little house area, they had people from six or seven families. No one knew how many people lived there, so no one ever provided enough food. So they were stealing the food to cook at the house. He never told anyone this. We didn't know how many people were really hungry there. Now we know, and we deliver more food to them."

Jackie's ability to allow the boy to feel comfortable and be honest—things people only do if they feel respected and dignified— led to a better outcome for a whole group of destitute community members. She is a great example of the importance of relationship building in food ministries.

About a year after our trip, civil unrest developed in Nicaragua over the government's handling of the nation's social security program. To protect her safety given that much of the protesting and associated government backlash involved college students and she looked so young, Jackie's family sent her to North Carolina while tensions remained high.

On a later trip to Pochocuape, I saw Jackie shortly after she had returned. She bravely shared with our group the challenges of being unmarried at her age in a gender-traditional society like Nicaragua and how her faith journey carried her through both her time away from home and the path on which she continued. The vulnerability she exhibited and the respect with which the group listened were fueled by the common faith we shared; trust and safety were assumed and provided.

On a much lighter note, during her time in North Carolina, Jackie's fluent English acquired a healthy southern accent, which she could dial up with the right amount of encouragement. There are few things cuter than hearing her shout, "Y'all need Jesus!" in a southern twang with a Latin accent.

8

Bye-Bye, Comfort Zone

After our time at Mateare, we returned to *Embajada del Cielo* for lunch. To say our group was a bit stunned would be like saying Niagara, New York, has a bit of a waterfall. The sentiment of "Did that really just happen?" was universal among the children and adults. Rone's objective to crack that shell early on so the soil is more fertile for the subsequent activities was accomplished, no doubt. But the day was far from over. Our collective faith walk was about to take another giant stride.

In my five decades on earth, I have washed exactly four pairs of feet: mine and those of my three children. (I can't even say I have washed Kelly's; she has a thing about feet.) You should also know that I don't get grossed out easily, including when it comes to feet. However, after lunch, when Rone gathered us in the compound's church and read from the Gospels about Jesus washing his disciples' feet, I developed a sinking feeling. If I were not still back on my heels from the morning outing, I might have detected the knowing glance between Rone and Jeff, both J-term veterans.

Rone finished speaking, and we exited the church onto the uneven concrete patio, where small weeds popped through the once-tight seams that time and tectonic progression had unzipped. Having never been this close to the equator, I was struck by the virtual absence of a shadow around my body; the sun was *directly* overhead. As my pupils completed their adjustment from the umbral church to the blazing sunlight, a line of blurry purple shapes materialized into a row of our Samaritans hosts seated in folding metal chairs. Further absorption of the scene revealed small, clear plastic bins in front of each person, filled halfway with water and swagged by white hand towels. The final detail was each staff member had removed their shoes and socks.

Gulp. I guess this was really going to happen—a clear opportunity to practice the rubber bracelet saying, "What would Jesus do?" There were more SWH missionaries than Samaritans staffers present, so I was paired with fellow chaperone Charles. We knelt before Josue, whose slightly widened eyes indicated he may have felt as sheepish as we did about the impending interaction. Charles had been on the prior year's J-term trip and, therefore, knew this was coming; I am not sure if I should have been upset he didn't tip me off or grateful he didn't ignite the pilot light on my dread sooner. First visiting a trash dump and now about to wash a total stranger's feet—bye-bye, comfort zone.

Washing Josue's feet consisted of pouring several handfuls of water over his smooth skin and using the towel to mop up the clinging drops. Charles cleaned his right foot, and I, his left. After helping him put his socks and shoes back on, we prayed together, giving thanks for the gift Josue and his coworkers would be in the days to come. We hugged, and the entirety of the group stood up, awkwardness replaced by amity.

Washing our Nicaraguan brother's feet—a process that took less than five minutes—moved me to the point where my eyes pooled. I stole away from the group for a few moments to collect and reflect. Reading *Leading with Dignity* by professor and conflict resolution expert Donna Hicks months later helped me understand my emotions in the moment: "We are all born worthy. Dignity is something we all deserve, no matter what we do. It is the starting point for the way we treat one another. . . . When we honor the dignity of others, it creates a sense of safety between us; people feel free to make themselves vulnerable, free to reveal their true selves. Relationships thrive when both parties feel they are seen, heard, and valued." The intimacy we shared and relationships we built with our hosts during those few minutes defy words. Our collective vulnerability was rewarded for doing what Jesus did.

I like the idea that dignity is connected to vulnerability and to intimacy. When I think about the closest relationships in my life, I know I am being a good version of myself when I am being vulnerable, dignifying others, and experiencing intimacy—emotional as well as physical.

My sister, Karen, was forty-two years old when she died in 2007. She was by herself at the time—called an "unattended death"—so an autopsy had to be performed. The official cause of death was "multiple drug intoxication—accidental." While she had a number of prescription and over-the-counter drugs in her system, all were within normal dosage levels except for Benadryl; its level was above normal but still significantly below what was considered a lethal dose. It was determined that a few of the substances contained various forms of neurological suppressants, and their combination shut down her nervous system.

Among the many devastating elements of losing my only sister and my parents' only daughter was that Karen died alone. Not just physically alone, but alone alone, as in no-one-was-really-close-to-her alone. She had never married, never found her soul mate, never had children. She had a big family, including many nieces and nephews—the orchard of her eye—and a diverse, eclectic group of friends. But each of these people—each of us—had our own inner relationship circles—spouses, partners, children—who collectively bumped Karen to the arc of an outer concentric circle. Kelli Harding says in *The Rabbit Effect* that "loneliness is like the killer lurking in the basement. . . . It's riskier than well-established hazards such as obesity, physical inactivity, high blood pressure, and bad cholesterol."

Emotional barriers and defense mechanisms separated Karen—a dynamic, intelligent, vivacious person—from deep, visceral relationships. From causes of both nature and nurture, Karen struggled with being vulnerable and therefore intimate—two feelings I believe show up only if someone feels dignified. Tragically, no one in this world can ever alter the path she walked; only God knows if her aloneness contributed to the way-too-premature end of her life. Through Karen I have felt—and still feel today, so many years later—how the absence of human dignity creates circumstances and relationships that do not feel at all human.

9

Pochocuape

After the washing of the feet and ensuing personal and group composure, our day 1 mission work continued. We were headed outside the compound to deliver food to and offer prayers for the surrounding community, a walking tour that was part goodwill but mostly good deed, as the local villagers lacked sufficient food to live. The delivery and distribution of food were and are a serious operation. Servants With a Heart sends their food from North Carolina to Nicaragua in forty-foot shipping crates that hold forty pallets, each of which carries thirty-three boxes, for a grand total of 1,320 boxes, or 285,120 meals. When logistics and customs are running smoothly, SWH ships eight to ten containers per year, which amounts to somewhere around two and a half million meals annually.

On this particular afternoon, the staff loaded food boxes onto two makeshift flatbed trailers pulled by donkeys. The trailers' outer frames consisted of two felled tree trunks, each about five inches in diameter. Lashed between them and forming the weight-bearing platform were somewhat even-length ratty floorboards of various thicknesses. One set of the ends of the trunks extended beyond the platform into a chain-link harness attached to the burros and cushioned by burlap blankets doubled over to bear the payload's weight across the animals' strong backs. Underneath the floor planks were homemade wooden strut-and-axle assemblies with ancient-looking tires, approximately fourteen inches in diameter. These transports were frugal, time tested, and seemingly reliable—and likely developed at a fraction of the cost a comparable store-bought wagon would be in the States.

The boxes were piled three high on the trailers and tethered down with well-worn tan and yellow ropes. It was fun to see the crayon and sharpie drawings and read the phrases on some of the boxes that the food-packing children back in the Carolinas had created. One of the J-termers found a box from a packing event in which she had participated the prior semester.

The Samaritans security guards pushed open the entry gate, its upper and lower channel grooves moaning in mild protest at the friction of metal on metal, and out we marched, ready to proffer the missionary one-two punch of physical and spiritual nourishment. Jeff and I joined the group heading right, into the heart of Pochocuape, while the others headed left, down the slope toward the hillside dwellings. Both groups had translators and security.

I was excited to be heading into the village, as Jeff had earlier told me about its baseball park, a sport bested by only soccer (*fútbol*) in popularity. I knew enough not to expect anything resembling a high school or municipal ball field from home; we were in a mountainside village in Nicaragua, miles from the city center. But what I saw as we emerged from the furrowed dirt road, closely enveloped by both palms and deciduous trees, was far from my expectations.

The "baseball park" consisted of a square clearing, perhaps forty yards across, with dirt and uneven splotches of crabgrass accounting for equal amounts of ground cover. There were faint suggestions of foul lines along two outer edges, which terminated in a large circular dirt clearing in the corner—home plate. Along what would be the third baseline and across the clearing in what would be right field stood *fútbol* goals, consisting of eight-foot-high posts and fifteen-foot-or-so cross bars of rusted pipe. There were no nets to catch the balls to indicate with certainty on which side of the pipe a shot had passed, surely the source of heated debates among local Messi and Ronaldo wannabes.

We crossed the field and plunged into an opening in the tree line barely wide enough for the trailer. The edges of the ensuing pass were lined with dense foliage, its thick greenery strengthening the moist tug of the lazy afternoon air. As we made our way into the thicket, a footpath appeared on our left, down which a structure emerged— our first home visit. The property line along the trail was girded by a two-strand barbed-wire fence with a broken gate that had once crossed the dirt entry path, down which I saw a few chickens pecking at the dust and a couple shirtless toddlers in worn athletic shorts waddling after them with sticks.

Beyond this front yard was a square structure, its blue wavy aluminum siding and dull gray roof standing perhaps fifteen feet long and ten feet high. Behind it to the left was a similar-size cinder block structure with a wooden roof. Chimneys billowing smoke rose out of the center of both homes, and between them, an open fire covered by a giant cast-iron kettle boiled water. Branches hung from ground level up to well over our heads, the homeowners using them to dry laundry and hang cooking utensils. In other communities later in the week, I would see extension cords strung along branches delivering power to lamps, transistor radios, and perhaps microwaves. In this part of Pochocuape—as throughout much of the developing world—there was no electricity.

Our Samaritans guide shouted a warm greeting to hail the adult residents. After a few moments, an elderly woman emerged from the aluminum dwelling. She was less than five feet tall and wore a stained white tank top, a holey blue wraparound skirt, and old flip-flops with the toe thongs flapping loose. Her gray hair was pulled back, exposing weathered cheeks and a wrinkled forehead. Her dark, deep-set eyes and slight smile conveyed a neighborly, maternal warmth that dissipated much of the anxiety I was unaware had built up inside me. This *abuelita* hobbled up to the fence line, where we waited respectfully. Our guide told her we had food and wanted to pray for her and her family. Her smile widened, exposing a lone tooth on the top and a few misaligned molars on the bottom, rising out of her gumline like stubborn rocks on an eroded jetty.

Our guide wanted to confirm how many people lived on the property; local knowledge is key, as most villagers are in need of food, and delivering appropriate quantities is critical (recall Jackie's story about the boy who was stealing). The woman said one family lived in each house, so we unloaded two boxes from the donkey cart. Each box weighs thirty-three pounds, a cumbersome load even for a man of my size. The abuelita raised her arms to receive a box, and I instinctively lunged into the exchange with my arms extended under hers, a forklift ready to catch the load that would surely drop. There was no way this diminutive woman had the strength to bear that weight.

Yet again my expectations were off. She took the box in her arms and absorbed its weight against her chest with relative ease, her facial expression barely changing. She sure-footed her way, broken sandals and all, back to her abode and placed the box inside before returning to our fence line meeting spot. No one emerged from the concrete structure, so one of our students carried a box to its door and placed it inside.

Now that the food had been delivered, a prayer would be offered. We sometimes lead with the food, sometimes with the Word; our guide chose the former in this instance. Because this was principally a trip for the Charlotte students, they were encouraged to say most of the prayers. One American girl asked the woman—via our interpreter—if she could pray for her and what she would like us to say. The abuelita's request foreshadowed many of the blessings we would bestow all week—a petition for health.

In most dwellings, three or four generations lived under one roof, sharing beds like the hodgepodge of grandparents in *Willy Wonka and the Chocolate Factory*, only more destitute. Someone was often homebound with one ailment or another. And it was safe to assume that everyone was nutrient deprived. The student's prayer—said in English and translated (being able to speak Spanish was not a requirement for the trip)—went something like this: "Dear Lord, thank you for the opportunity to distribute these blessings. Please bless this family and this food to help their bodies and bring them health. Amen." Not too shabby, particularly seeing as most American teenagers avoid effective communications in their own homes, let alone out here in the Nicaraguan mountainside . . . to total strangers . . . through an interpreter.

I believe this woman's petition for health went beyond the physical sort. These villagers—particularly the matriarchs—were committed to the role of family custodian and nurturer. Beyond bodily well-being, I suspect some knew that education, like Samaritans International offered in their school, and opportunities to acquire skills and knowledge could provide the right centrifugal force to propel their children out of the vicious cycle of poverty and despair. I believe they knew that the hope and faith that come from spiritual health could undergird their collective willpower in ways even food could not.

The balance of the afternoon was much the same, delivering boxes of food, interacting with the very young to the very old, and praying, our intercessions feeling more natural and sincere with each passing family. The Spanish I had learned in high school and college started to reemerge, as we adults interacted with the villagers and offered a few blessings as well. My vocabulary was limited, and my verb conjugation was surely off, but I could convey and absorb the intent of the conversations; true communications need not involve actual words, let alone proper tense or grammar.

The chance to interact, even for a few moments, to establish a human connection—touch, words, eye contact, kneeling down to a child's height so she knows she matters—can warm people's hearts and imprint their memory banks long after a five-minute *hola*-to-*adios* interaction concludes. Jimmy, our Samaritans host who had picked me up at the airport, summarized how these routine acts have a profound impact. "For me, that's what it means to be part of a mission team. Out there in the communities, there's people that appreciate that you show up and share hope and love. You give hugs and just talk to them, ask their name. It means a lot." I agree; it seemed to mean a lot to the villagers—and to us.

Connecting the routine to the profound reminds me of a conversation with a coworker back in my late twenties. I was telling him (okay, I was boasting) about Kelly being an elementary school teacher. I was spouting about how she was shaping young lives, laying the academic, intellectual, and moral foundations Robert Fulghum enumerates in *All I Really Needed to Know I Learned in Kindergarten*. I concluded by suggesting what my colleague and I did (accounting and sales, respectively) paled in comparison to Kelly's vocation. Without missing a beat, he retorted, passionately noting how the duties we performed supported thousands of workers around the country, who, in turn, could provide food for their families, pay their mortgages, and feel good about themselves. Such a chain of connections, like capacitors and relays in an electrical circuit, was not evident to me at the time, and I remain grateful to my coworker for pointing it out.

That early career exchange about the value of an occupation—particularly for how it fuels self-worth—ignited in me a lifelong belief in the dignity of work. There are few things in my experience that stoke someone's self-esteem better than knowing that he or she is performing tasks that support or improve society. *I am good at my job. I am rewarded for what I do. I can provide for myself and others. What I do matters.* Too often people feel uninspired or disengaged because they don't see the connection between their efforts—at work, at home, in the community—and the greater purpose of an organization or cause.

This belief is one of the reasons I have cherished spending much of my career in the staffing industry, where the principal objective is to fill clients' open positions with qualified workers. We are occupational matchmakers, helping businesses achieve their goals and professionals earn both income and dignity. What does dignity look like in what you do? Walking through Pochocuape that afternoon, I got a glimpse of it—through the eyes of an abuelita nurturing her family.

10

Mouths of Babes

Back at the compound, I took a much-needed shower, my first interaction with the widowmaker proceeding without incident. We all then assembled for dinner. Folks were tired; it had been a loooong day—physically, emotionally, spiritually. Despite our collective exhaustion, there was a palpable buzz. Our shared experiences—trash dump, feet washing, village walk—fueled our spirits and built our *esprit de corps*. As you may have surmised, I am a pretty major extrovert so was particularly tapped into the group vibe.

We gathered later for our first evening debrief, the daily exercise Rone had introduced the night before. Rone, Jeff, Charles, and I met with the boys, while Dena Brown, the lone female chaperone, and one of the Samaritans female guides took the girls. Dena (pronounced "dee-na") is a married mother of three, one of whom was on the trip. She operates her own business and also founded Mercy Matters, a Charlotte-based nonprofit focused on providing water, food, and other necessities to families in need in the Carolinas and abroad. Dena had short blonde hair, big blue eyes, and a bright smile that lit up any conversation she joined. She wore her faith on her sleeve. I liked her from the moment I met her.

The task for each of us that night was to list the main events and activities from the day that had a significant impact. The instructions asked us to "keep in mind that God works in unique ways, and what may be significant for one team member may not be for another." This was a reminder about the spiritual nature of our trip and that each of our journeys would be unique.

The boys in our group offered up various anecdotes from the day, many of which were unknown to me, given the variety and dispersion of our efforts. Our most poignant discussion centered on our shared encounter with María. Her faith was staggering, her perspective humbling. After everyone echoed similar feelings of awe, the following exchange occurred between two of the boys:

"Wow. It's amazing that she said she was happy. Just incredible. I mean, with how little she had, she felt like that? Just think how she would feel if she had everything we have."

Without missing a beat, the other boy countered, "She wouldn't be happy."

I'm not sure if my jaw dropped open, but my eyes certainly teared up. Just one day removed from the creature comforts of home, and there was already a realization that material things may not be so material.

Reflecting on this exchange, Charles offered, "I can't imagine an average kid being able to speak like those children did that first night. I mean, I'm in my fifties, and I know I can't."

Both the Old Testament (in the book of Psalms) and the New Testament (in Matthew's Gospel) talk about wisdom coming "from the mouths of babes." Devotional writer Oswald Chambers notes the spiritual clarity with which young people view life, unbridled by the years of worldly filters and jaded perspectives we adults have amassed. "A complete life is the life of a child . . . A child of God is not aware of the will of God because he is the will of God . . . A child of God never prays to be made aware of the fact that God answers prayer, because he is so restfully certain that God always answers prayer." Might this sound like youthful naïveté? In part, maybe. But I believe such conviction is a key faith tenet allowing us humans to know we are not on our own.

On a related note, I recall one morning many years ago driving my daughter to nursery school when she exhibited her own youthful faith. With no context and no warning, she chirped from her booster seat behind me, "Daddy, do you think God wears clothes?" *What? Did I hear her right? Think fast! Think fast! Oh right—redirect!* So I replied, "Gee, honey, I don't know. What do you think?" She paused for a moment and with steadfast consideration responded, "I don't know either. I used to think 'no,' but now I'm not sure." From the mouths of babes, indeed.

We adults spend so much of our time and energy focused on *teaching* children, we miss opportunities to *learn* from them and their recurring enjoyment of life's routine. My time with those J-term teenagers reminded me of this two-way street, something I strive to appreciate more with my own family.

The first time I encountered the concept of dignity was during my time at Landmark, in my early twenties. The people I met during my brief experience there were a true slice of Americana—racially, socioeconomically, every-other-way-ly. I realized that, despite our surface and descriptive differences, we shared common desires and aspirations, as well as fears and insecurities. Much of the latter centered on wanting to be valued and wanting to belong.

I recall one conversation with a gay man not much older than me; he shared the vulnerability he was feeling in his relationship, worried he might not be good enough for his partner. What has stuck with me—and I'll preface this by acknowledging my conservative upbringing—is not only was I having one of my first substantive conversations with a person whose sexual orientation differed from mine but that he experienced the same relationship worries I did (and in some ways, still do).

I wonder about Christianity's take on sexual orientation. A common interpretation of the Bible, shared by many forms of Protestantism and by official Roman Catholic doctrine, is homosexuality is a sin, that man and woman were created to complement each other and existing otherwise is ungodly. But I struggle with the universality of this belief. With each successive lap I make around the sun, I believe more strongly we are all created in God's image, and all of us—straight and queer—are loved and deserve to have our dignity recognized and honored. I do not accept that gay men and women are somehow less in the eyes and in the heart of God. I literally cannot imagine the challenges faced by the LGBTQ community. As a person of faith called to be in relationship with all of God's creation, I still have much discerning and learning to do and much dialogue to have to become comfortable and confident as an agent of God's love and an ally for all people to be their whole selves.

Near the conclusion of one of the Landmark seminars, the participants were asked to compose a personal life vision, sort of a compass for your path forward that had personal resonance. In hindsight I can see the prescient nature of mine, as it centered on the belief that every human being has dignity. I do not recall why the concept of dignity resonated for me then, nor did I know that twenty-some years later I would devote several chapters of a book to it. My time in Nicaragua brought this life vision back into focus. What could be more central than honoring another person? Is there a stronger expression of love?

As if our first full day in Nicaragua was not action-packed enough, that night was the national title game for college football back in the States, and one of Charlotte Christian's graduates was playing for the Georgia Bulldogs. As a surreal but comforting bookend to our day, Rone and the Samaritans team had conjured a Wi-Fi-enabled feed of the game, which was projected onto a wall in the back right corner of the dormitory portion of the compound. They secured Latin American variations of US sodas and salty snacks, mandatory sustenance when two or more gather to watch a sporting event. Appropriately, the American commentators' voices were occasionally replaced by a Spanish broadcast. While the Alabama Crimson Tide bested the Bulldogs by a field goal, it was fun to see the students cheer on a former schoolmate. But it was also a tad strange to enjoy a comfort of home after a day spent so far out of my comfort zone.

Part 3

TUESDAY: TALENTS

What's God's plan for the whole world?
Buckle up! It's us.

—BOB GOFF, *Love Does*

11

If Jesus Were You

By Tuesday morning, it felt like we were starting to hit our stride, like a peloton of riders on a long flat-road trek. Our *Embajada* breakfasts each day consisted of either scrambled eggs or omelets, along with some form of pork product, a starchy potato or flour concoction, fresh fruit, and cereal—a substantial, well-balanced tankful to start our mission day and another example of the juxtaposition of our fare and the food insecurity surrounding the compound. I was starting to recognize the cadre of women in the kitchen area off the dining area who cranked out our meals, as well as (I presume) a few of their young children who flitted between the tables and in and out of the front door to the courtyard.

Over coffee I had my first opportunity to chat with Erling, Patrick's second-in-command at Samaritans and the coordinator of our day-to-day efforts. A native Nicaraguan in his late thirties or early forties, Erling was thick-chested and seemed to carry his weight well. As a lifelong Philadelphia Eagles fan, I did not appreciate the Dallas

Cowboys T-shirt he wore, but at least we shared an affinity for the NFL. Under his Nike Swoosh khaki baseball cap (another sign of US culture's permeation), Erling's thick eyebrows crested over warm eyes and a room-brightening smile that exposed a full set of perfectly straight teeth. He spoke fluent English with an accent that was neither mild nor severe. His voice reminded me of what John Steinbeck wrote about the character Slim in *Of Mice and Men*: "His tone was friendly. It invited confidence without demanding it."

Erling had joined Samaritans eight years earlier after a life of ups and downs. As a teenager and young adult, he said he was not a great person. "I used to fight in the streets. I don't even know how many people I used to fight with. I didn't know about love, about peace, about faith, about God." He started selling mobile phones and eventually had his own business, a lucrative venture in a hot market. He also fell in love and got married. Then life's roller coaster again turned down. "I was making good money, every single day. I thought I was in the right place. I thought I was happy. Then one day, I lost everything I had. No job, no money, nothing. I was home, and my wife was pregnant."

Providence shone on him, however, when a neighbor who worked as a part-time maintenance person at *Embajada del Cielo* asked Erling if he would like to come to the compound for three days' work. Those three days of gardening and trash disposal turned into five days and then two weeks and, eventually, eight years. Erling had found his calling: "This place was a blessing in my life. When I came here, I found peace. I found love. I found kindness and learned how to show it to the people that really need it. It's really, really amazing how God can show you the plan for your life. I love this Samaritans family and all the people that come to serve our people. I love what I do."

I was impressed by Erling's candor despite just making my acquaintance; immediate transparency like this was not something I experienced often. While I had had a few meaningful conversations so far on the trip, this was the first time I named what was going on: Erling was showing up as a *brother in Christ*, someone with whom I shared a common faith and could therefore dive deep and be vulnerable from the outset.

And it was clear that his faith journey had revealed to him the talents he possessed, the gifts of his personality and skill set that he could share with coworkers and those to whom he ministered. Talents and gifts—each of us has a unique set of them, what we were given and what we have developed. One of the most important and gratifying tasks in life is discovering what our talents are and how we are supposed to use them to make a difference.

After breakfast, sunscreen application, and the proof-of-life photoshoot, we again loaded into the cage truck and departed down the hill out of Pochocuape (more chaperone shouts of "Tree!" and "Duck!"). Today we were heading about an hour away, to a community that was a regular site for Samaritans International's work. Once we descended the mountain and entered a highway, Jeff told us to expect to see a hundred or more children, ranging from the very young to our kids' ages. Jeff's words set the tone for the responsibility—and opportunity—our group would have: "Think about those kids you'll see there. Most of you don't know their language. So how do you build a connection? How do you build a relationship just to put a smile on someone's face for today?" I think we all found this preconditioning helpful as we pulled up next to the church that anchored the remote community.

Iglesia Lirio de los Valles, or Church of Lily of the Valley, is a Pentecostal place of worship, which are common across the global south. Pentecostal faiths put a high emphasis on the Holy Spirit, believing that the power of the Spirit inhabits believers. In many regions like Latin America, whose precolonial religions involved omnipresent spirits (good and evil), Christianity morphed to this format to appeal to uninitiated locals. Jeff and Suzanne informed me how many Pentecostal churches are considered "charismatic," which—as the name implies—means they employ visible signs and outward displays of worship, including a lot of physical movement and even speaking in tongues.

Given the aforementioned Spanish colonial roots of the country, Nicaragua's majority Christian population is mostly Roman Catholic, but many practice various forms of Protestantism as well, a key difference being that Protestants believe scripture should predominantly dictate one's beliefs and practices, whereas Catholics combine biblical teachings with apostolic tradition, which is the Church's scriptural interpretations and expressions of faith. Patrick would later explain how the various denominations in Nicaragua do not always see eye to eye, and Samaritans International had to be careful to know which form of religion the people to whom they ministered practiced. This us-versus-them divisiveness within Christianity has influenced my personal faith journey, most notably fueling my afore-mentioned belief in a big tent when it comes to religion.

The church was large, perhaps a hundred feet long and forty-some feet wide. Its concrete walls were light blue with large wrought-iron-covered openings on the front and sides. There was a line of thin palm trees along each side wall, their fronds rising above the sloped roof to provide additional shade beyond the narrow eave. The first four feet or so of each trunk were painted the same light blue as the church walls, providing protection for the wood and the ancillary benefit of color coordination.

Entering the church I noticed the exposed steel rafters, their crisscross pattern and deliberate spans of separation leading me to wonder about the structural calculations that dictated their design, the latest reminder that I was the only one of my brothers *not* to study engineering in college. A few simple light fixtures with exposed bulbs hung from the rafters; this location had electricity. The room was spacious, absent the pews or fixed seating you would typically see in North American churches. The floor consisted of one-foot-square tiles, which indicated the quality and purpose of the building; most church floors were natural dirt. All the tiles had a swirly brown-and-white pattern except a three-tile-wide tan pathway leading from the entry area down the middle of the church to the altar, a wooden platform about eighteen inches high that was backed by large white and red curtains swagged across each other in decorative crescents. On the left side of the altar ("stage right" in theater speak) were a keyboard, a drum set, music stands, and stools, equipment standing ready to glorify God with melody and harmony.

Reflecting on the experience of entering that large room, I think about church doors. They function like any doors do, opening and closing to allow or restrict access. But the doors of a house of worship convey a symbolic message as well, a two-way meaning. Open or closed, a doorway invites strangers to share in the grace of God with the community of the faithful . . . or not. And, open or closed, doors signal to those inside to go out and meet others where they are in the world . . . or not. On this day—and throughout this week—the church doors were wide open, drawing people both into the safe and nurturing sanctuary and out into the varying and at times cruel world.

Positioned in two concentric ovals around the outer portions of the room were white plastic chairs, filled with the hundred or so children Jeff told us about on the drive. I was struck by how calm and well-behaved the kids were, particularly the littlest ones sitting toward the center of the group. There were a few adults, again mostly women, standing around the outside of the ovals. Our SWH group, clad today in gray T-shirts, entered the large opening in the middle of the crowd and huddled together a tad nervously—well, I was nervous anyway—proverbial fish in a fish bowl.

One by one, however, our group branched out and engaged with the children, a few of the more outgoing students leading the way. Samaritans musicians—who I later learned had arrived ahead of us to set up the bandstand—began playing music, which predictably lightened the mood. Eventually all of us fanned out into the still-seated children and began to interact. The person who struck me the most during this melding of nationality and culture was Jeff's good friend Charles. I caught him out of the corner of my eye kneeling on the hard tile so he was eye to eye with two boys, maybe six and ten years old. I could not hear what he was saying (and of course the boys could not understand his English), but Charles's eye contact and gesturing, including large shoulder shrugs and fist waving, had their rapt attention, their forward-leaning posture and wide grins serving as telltales of their enthrallment. *Attaboy, Charles!*

After several minutes of these ice-breaking interactions, our high schoolers were organized in the middle of the opening and asked to perform a song. By "perform," I don't mean "sing" (that would be done by a Samaritans staff member) but actually perform—act out the lyrics of the song as translated to them. This would be my first introduction to "*Había un Sapo*" ("There Was a Toad"), an animated children's song about a frog during which the performers bounce around to the music and do their best to act like a frog. It is quite catchy, and the returning J-termers performed it particularly well, bringing joy to the wide-eyed children seated around them.

After the song and dance, our leaders ushered everyone outside to the adjacent field, where the magnet of all universal magnets was waiting: a soccer ball—several of them, in fact. These were the same mission balls we had used the day before at Mateare. Instantaneously preteen Nicaraguan boys began dribbling in front of their larger, older guests, showing off their skills and luring the Americans into one-on-one battles. The locals all wore long pants, yet none broke out in sweat like the shorts-adorned North Carolina kids did, an indication of how the human body adapts to its climate.

Under a group of tall trees off to one side of the field were a few chairs and boxes of toys we had brought with us. I sat down, as did Dena, our faith-on-her-sleeve chaperone. Some of the boxes contained necklace- and bracelet-making kits with colored string, beads, and animal-shaped trinkets. As we would do at each of our community visits, many of our group made jewelry with the local kids, creating lasting mementos of our brief interactions. The box between Dena and me contained temporary tattoos—lots and lots of temporary tattoos. While most of the older kids, especially the boys, gravitated to the large soccer match that was now organizing, a surprising and somewhat intimidating number of younger kids formed two lines in front of us, ready for ink.

The process of wiping the skin (mostly cheeks but a few forearms and hands), moistening the tattoo, applying it, and—most importantly—knowing how long to hold it in place before the all-or-nothing peel of the paper—is relatively easy, something I did dozens of times as a kid at the Jersey Shore. In this instance, however, with dozens of eager youngsters in line and high humidity making skin preparation challenging, the time required to complete the process seemed eternal. The repetitive task enabled me to hone my Spanish by asking the same questions over and over: ¿Cómo estás? (How are you?), ¿Qué tal? (What's up?), ¿Cómo te llamas? (What is your name?), ¿Qué tatuaje quieres? (What tattoo do you want?), ¿Te gusta? (Do you like it?). Many of our exchanges ended with a hug, a closing gesture Dena practiced more than me.

While our garbled Spanglish exchanges with the children were meaningful ways to connect, there was a different energy when we made eye contact, a chance perhaps to glimpse into one another's soul. Our physical touch was equally special: wiping cheeks, holding forearms, applying tattoos, hugging. Platonic physical touch conveys our humanness and our humaneness in ways that glances and words cannot. Contact is essential for true connection, for universal cultural- and generational-spanning relationships. Touch is central to love. And love, like faith, is a contact sport; you have to be in motion, interacting with others, to express your affection and offer your talents and gifts.

Salt is referenced in Christianity, Judaism, Islam, and Hinduism as an important symbol. Over centuries it has had many uses—a seasoning for food, a preservative for meats, and even a healing agent for physical ailments. But salt is worthless by itself. It has to interact with—touch—the food or the person to have effect. The same holds true for love and affection and how we help each other through our life journeys and our faith journeys.

The most memorable moment of my hour (yup, an hour) of tattoo application was with a young boy whose name sadly escapes me. His head was wrapped in a bandage, although I could not tell what injury he had. What made him memorable was the Unionville Lacrosse reversible tank top he wore. It is not uncommon to see logoed clothes from the States in other countries, given the number of churches and community organizations that send used clothing overseas. What made this boy's shirt memorable was that Unionville is less than an hour from my home (two thousand miles from our pop-up tattoo parlor), and my son's good friend played lacrosse there. Bizarre. I had Dena snap a photo of the two of us (I wasn't cool enough to take a selfie), which I sent home.

As our supplies ran empty—I'll be honest, I was happy when they did—my hands were quite pruned, the ruts and wrinkles on fingers and palms reminiscent of nightly childhood bath time. It was tiring, but I felt a heightened connection to the place, having interacted with so many kids and now seeing all those newly colored cheeks and hands scurrying about.

Speaking of hands—and the body more broadly—reflecting on our time with the children makes me think again about one of my favorite faith concepts: talents. Like Erling, each of us has unique talents and gifts, just like each part of our body serves a unique and special purpose. We have been given and can develop these talents to help others, doing our unique part to make the world a better place. "For as in one body, we have many parts, and all the parts do not have the same function, so we, though many, are one body in Christ and individually parts of one another. Since we have gifts that differ according to the grace given to us, let us exercise them" (Romans 12:4–6). I like the concept that, like body parts, we are all related and interrelated, both to God and to each other, from the largest bones and organs to the smallest. In college, I could not walk after breaking the fifth metatarsal along the outer edge of my foot (a pretty tiny bone) so can attest to how, when even one of the smallest parts of your body does not do its job, the whole body is compromised.

The most well-known biblical reference to talents is the parable of, well, the talents. In this story, a master goes on a journey. While he is gone, he entrusts his servants with his talents, which, in this context, means a large unit of currency. He gives each servant a different amount based on their capabilities. When the master returns, the two servants who were given higher sums had handled the talents wisely, returning even more money than they were given. But the one who was given the least did nothing with his allotment; he buried it in the ground instead of investing it or in some other way using it for good. The master punishes him and rewards his sum to the servant who returned the most.

The message I take is that whatever capability you have, your central duty as a person of faith is to exercise that capability (i.e., talent) to the fullest, not bury it in the ground and do nothing. I heard a sermon once where the preacher referenced an American philosopher named Dallas Willard, who said that our purpose in life is "to become who Jesus would be if He were you." Willard didn't say our purpose is to *become Jesus*. No. It is to become whom He would be *if He were us*; each of us should use the talents and gifts we have been given—and have developed—to help others.

I like this idea. We are not tasked to do the extraordinary. We are tasked to apply what we have in the situations in which we find ourselves. Helping each other is ministry, not the pulpit/preachy kind but the employing-our-talents-and-gifts kind. In Dena's and my case on this day, that meant applying tattoos to Nicaraguan children until our hands pruned. With how busy and complicated and sometimes really hard life can be, I find comfort in the notion that my real task is to find out what unique things I can offer and then offer them. No more is asked. What if we all did this, these rather ordinary tasks, often in ordinary situations? That, my friends, would be extraordinary.

But we are conditioned to ask more of ourselves. We overschedule ourselves and our loved ones, overcommitting and overextending. And we prioritize the appearance of being in control, even when we are not. If we are being honest, don't we often feel ineffective, like there is never enough time? Maybe twenty-four hours is, in fact, the perfect length for a day, and we are just bad at calibrating our expectations?

Speaking of time and how we use it, recall how I had earlier spotted Charles on his knees acting animatedly in front of those kids. I asked him later about that moment. He said, "I feel like maybe it had real meaning. I can't help but think either their dads are not around or maybe they're in a field fourteen hours a day or something.

I wonder if there's ever been some old foreign guy who's played with them like that. Whether that's a Christian thing or just a human being thing, I don't know. But I'd like to think it had some kind of lingering effect. I know it did on me." Powerful words from my brother's good friend, a man with a huge heart—and also a man who later in the week would act like both *un pollo* (a chicken) and *un gato* (a cat) for the amusement of dozens of strangers—a long way from his corporate executive persona back in Baltimore.

12

God's Instrument

As the soccer playing, beading, and tattooing wrapped up, I
could smell food cooking next to a small building at the far
end of the field . . . my first chance to deliver prepared meals
to these beautiful people I was just starting to appreciate. Samaritans
traveled with a giant wok-shaped pot, perhaps four feet across, and
a large propane-powered burner for heating water, into which the
packets of SWH food were placed and cooked.

Each bag of food contained six balanced meals of rice, soy, dried
vegetables, and vitamins and minerals, and each box contained
thirty-six bags, for a total of two hundred and sixteen servings. Each
serving had been assembled based on nutritional recommendations
for the people who would consume it, its two hundred and twenty calories designed to provide sustenance well beyond what an equivalent
calorie meal in an American kitchen would. The wok had a full box
of food simmering, the hot water bringing to life the nutrients and
pleasing aroma of food packed in churches and schools back at home.

With the fragrance drifting across the field, everyone filed back into the church, the children back to their seats and we J-termers standing in a ring behind them. Again, I noticed how sweaty we Americans were and how much water we consumed (remember those wasteful 16.9-ounce plastic bottles?), while the local children had hardly broken a sweat or taken a sip. Did we Americans have so much water available because we knew we would be thirsty, or were we thirsty because we knew we would have so much water available?

With everyone back together, the newly formed bonds between Nicaraguans and Americans palpable, one of our boys made his way to the altar and was handed a microphone. This would be my first experience hearing someone give their testimony. Being raised in an Episcopalian church in a fairly conservative community and worshiping much of my adult life with Kelly at Catholic churches, my lifetime Christian experience was staid, with reverent, orderly congregations reciting prayer book passages and singing mostly historical hymns.

The experience of hearing people give their testimonies—essentially a three-part story of their life before finding Jesus, the moment at which they discovered Jesus and accepted Him as Lord and Savior, and what their life has been like since—was as foreign to me as many of the other (actually) foreign aspects of the trip. In fact, I did not even pick up on the structure of these speeches until the end of the week. Again, I was hearing and learning from the mouths of "babes."

What this young man offered in his testimony, as many of the high schoolers and even a few of the adults would as the week unfolded, was inspiring, and it was humbling. Over the coming days the kids would talk about parents getting divorced, falling sick themselves and being bedbound for long periods of time, even losing a parent at a young age. For most, those events tested their spiritual resolve, even in one or two cases causing them to question God's existence or walk away from their faith. But all of them, along his or her unique path, found their way back—so much so that they got on that plane a few days earlier to fly a long distance to minister to kids and families they had never met or even considered.

After the testimony, which Jackie from Samaritans translated for the locals, Patrick, our leader, walked into the center of the room, accompanied by Jimmy, my airport driver from Sunday, and one of Patrick's daughters. Like other US missionaries I met, Patrick had married a Nicaraguan (after he and his wife with whom he moved to Nicaragua got divorced). His wife is named Carolina (the I is pronounced like a long E). This trio—Patrick, Jimmy, and Patrick's daughter—was assembling for the preaching portion of our visit. Patrick was about to convey the biblical account from Mark's Gospel of Jesus reviving a girl whose parents thought she had died. Patrick spoke decent Spanish—more than enough to get by—but he was having Jimmy translate in this instance. Patrick had his daughter slouch down in a chair in the middle of the room, her legs sprawled out before her and her arms flopped out straight over each arm rest. She threw her head back, and he placed a towel over her face. She lay motionless, play acting the presumably dead daughter.

Patrick—with Jimmy translating—started speaking slowly and deliberately, setting the scene for the children. As the story unfolded, his voice rose and fell along steeper and steeper sound waves, and he skulked around the opening with Jimmy in shadowlike lockstep, translating Patrick's words and mimicking his tonal inflections. Their synchronous prowling around the open oval conjured images of jungle cats eyeing their next meal. The kids—and we—were spellbound.

Patrick's orating got louder and more animated, and he gyrated his arms and used a rag to wipe the increasing beads of sweat from his upper lip and bald head, the hundred-plus people in the church increasing the already sultry midday heat. The climax of the story was when Jesus commanded the girl to awaken, which she did, to the surprise and joy of her parents . . . and of dozens of wide-eyed children in the church. Pretty intense. And pretty cool.

Meanwhile, at one point during the preaching, an American man with our group, wearing neither an SWH nor a Samaritans shirt, ran past me and out the door, sobbing. I was so fixed on the trio in the ring that I did not process his passing until afterward. Apparently the emotion of the moment triggered something, and he left the church to collect himself. I later heard (secondhand from Jeff, I think) that the man was living and working at *Embajada* for a few weeks while he "got his life back in order"; at various times a few "lost souls" from the US would make their way down to Pochocuape to work with—and be ministered by—Patrick as they sorted out various addiction, financial, or relationship challenges. Lost sheep, in need of a shepherd.

At this point in the day (keep in mind it wasn't even lunchtime), Rone's "seeds of faith" and "fertile ground" from the previous afternoon were initiating a spiritual germination inside of me. I guess that was preparing me for what was next.

With the dead girl back to life, Patrick composed himself, his purple polo shirt soaked through, and invited us sojourners into the oval. He announced that we were missionaries from *los Estados Unidos* who came to pray for them. He explained how far we had traveled. He then asked the local kids and the few adults in the room to come to the center if they wanted someone to pray for them. He asked them to think about what they wanted to pray for and said that we missionaries would ask God for it.

I was shocked at how many children stood up and entered the opening; Patrick was using his talent of preaching and being an instrument of God. At this point, my heart was pounding and my mind was racing. *To whom would I walk? What would I ask them?*

Would I have the courage to pray in Spanish or summon one of the Samaritans translators to facilitate? (I opted for the latter.) I ended up with a little boy who asked me to pray for his family, which I did. I repeated this course of action—approach, inquire, pray—with a few other children and also joined a couple group prayers, some led by our kids and some by Patrick and his staffers.

Through these prayer sessions I was exposed to two missionary practices. First, when you pray for someone like we did, you lay your hands *on* them—on their head, their shoulders, or their back or maybe one hand on their head and one holding their hand. Unbeknownst to me, the laying *on* of hands is employed in many forms of religion, from Christianity to the Native American Navajo tradition. Again I experienced the power of touch, both as intimate connector and energy transmitter.

The second concept I gleaned from our prayer session was the idea that we prayed both *for* people and *over* them. Praying *for* someone makes sense; we say this phrase all the time: *Please pray* for *me. Please pray for my father. Let's all pray for the victims.* In several Christian denominations' church services, the congregation will offer Prayers of the People or Prayers of the Faithful, a series of intercessions for world and church leaders, the destitute, the sick, and the deceased, among others. Each petition may be followed by a group recitation like "Lord, hear our prayer."

On a side note, whenever I hear this phrase (*Lord, hear our prayer*), I wonder, if God is all-knowing, doesn't that include being all-hearing, and therefore not in need of being asked to *hear* our prayer? Isn't it a bit redundant to ask? As I have become more focused on my faith journey in recent years, I find myself questioning phrases like this, even though I have recited them my whole life; I am more engaged in—and therefore more accountable for—my spiritual life. Unlike praying *for* people, the idea of praying *over* them conveyed a different sense, that by being "over" them we were channeling good-will (literally) from above.

The practices of laying on of hands and praying over someone hit me in an emotional way, seeing how the people in the church concentrated on our words and embraced us when we finished. As we concluded the prayers, I realized something . . . I was *a missionary*—literally a missionary. I was there to bless and nurture these believers, and they believed what I said mattered. They were God's followers, and I was God's instrument. This was a first for me, and I cried at the gravity of the moment.

The realization brought back a lot of what I had read prior to the trip, most notably Livermore's *Serving with Eyes Wide Open*, the subtitle of which is *Doing Short-Term Missions with Cultural Intelligence*. Livermore writes about "the changing face of Christianity," saying that the largest Christian communities today are not in the US or Europe but in Africa and Latin America; none of the world's fifty largest Christian churches is in the States. As such, the "typical" profile of a modern-day Christian is not someone like me but "young, poor, theologically conservative, female, and a person of color." This was news to me and my myopic religious worldview. Christianity is the fastest-growing religion as well, with worldwide growth rates close to 7 percent as opposed to rates in the 2 to 3 percent range for Islam, Hinduism, and Buddhism.

Beyond religious topics, Livermore writes that, of the more than two billion children in the world, half live in poverty, and one-quarter have to work instead of attend school. Piling on epidemics of disease, a lack of potable water, and infant mortality rates, Livermore's writings foreshadowed a pivotal opportunity: As missionaries—as instruments—we J-termers were embodying a well-known passage from one of the major prophets of the Old Testament, Isaiah: "Then I heard the voice of the Lord saying, 'Whom shall I send? Who will go for us?' 'Here I am,' I said; 'send me!'" (Isaiah 6:8). We were there as the hands and feet—and hearts and minds—of God. This realization was awesome, both in the "whoa, that's cool" sense and in the "this is a lot to handle" sense.

Over the course of the week, I had the chance to ask others what doing mission work meant to them. Jeff offered that "you hear from everybody that goes on these trips that they just feel closer to God. I don't know whether it's the distractions of home, whether it be the United States or anywhere else, or if it's distractions of the wealth and all the stuff we have. But I think there's a pure conduit to God on these trips." Dena seconded this sentiment: "I think there is this deep desire to feel closer to God, and then you go and you do [feel closer]."

Rone called it a moral compass check. He said, "We live in South Charlotte, have access to private schools, country clubs, all that stuff—all the materialism. You get caught up in that stuff pretty easy, and you get sucked into it. It's important to have a compass check, to assess yourself every so often, to realize you don't need a lot of stuff to be happy. Coming here gives a reference point for first-world problems. Maybe I don't need that car, or I don't need that house or whatever that material thing is. Here, you find happiness and purpose."

I was again reminded of María from Mateare, that happiness can come in all forms—perhaps the less material, the better.

Even after two trips to Nicaragua, Charles professes not to be deeply religious, certainly relative to the likes of Jeff, Dena, and Rone. So in some ways, his reflections carried more weight.

"I came last year for the first time," he said, "because my best friend [Jeff] had started this journey, and I had gone to all these packing events and had always enjoyed them. Then one night I thought, *Okay, where is this food going?* And soon after, Jeff emails me saying I should get down to Nicaragua. So I did what made the most sense: I ignored his email. But he's Jeff, so he sent another email and then another. Before I knew it, it was like six weeks before last year's trip, and I said, 'I think I'll go.' Meanwhile, the whole trip's already planned, but Jeff said, 'Sure.' To be honest, though, even when I landed in Dallas for my connecting flight to come here, I still wasn't convinced I would go. I hadn't done anything like this, ever."

Charles's candor and vulnerability were inspiring. I could relate so well, both to how he felt and to the sequence of events. Jeff had been inviting me for years before I accepted. Something I did not appreciate then but do now is how we both ended up there. At the time, I would have said it was all about Jeff's enthusiasm and about Charles and me making similar but unrelated decisions. But today, I attribute this to the Holy Spirit, to the work of God's invisible hand steering us to where we can help fulfill my favorite phrase from the Lord's Prayer: "Thy will be done."

Charles continued the account of his first trip the prior year, explaining how his comfort zone was tested: "And then I got here, and I'm a pretty reserved person. So the whole thing about getting into people's space, getting involved with them, it was just weird for me. Why would someone want me to come there to do this? Wouldn't it be embarrassing for them to have me give them food? I gotta say, I was more than marginally uncomfortable. I would try to force myself to do a little of it, but it was much more comfortable for me to unload the truck, carry boxes, things that were needed but not interactive. None of them involved hugging a seven-year-old kid.

"But by the end of the trip, it was different. I was only here five days or something, but by the end, it was more comfortable. I got to feeling like, *Well, this really isn't that strange, and I am here for a reason.* I would send messages back home, emails or texts. And by the end of the week, people were responding like, 'You seem different. Your messages sound different.'

"I got home, and it kind of changed my whole life. It changed the way I thought about the world and the way I did things. So returning this year was a nondecision. I really missed being here. Coming back was easy."

And to think, it was the kids who were supposed to be growing spiritually.

Both students and chaperones benefited from our interactions with the locals, reinforcing my earlier rhetorical question about who was ministering to whom. Erling, Patrick's second-in-command, had spent eight years at Samaritans, so he had seen hundreds of American teens come and go, experiencing firsthand how they grew during their missions.

"On the first day, all the time, the American kids are a little bit shy. The next day, they start walking around and joking and playing with a few of the community kids. But by the end of the week, it's often hard to get them out from the villages because they don't want to leave the children. In all the years I have worked here, I saw a lot of kids, American kids, crying when we go to the communities, because they see how tough life is. They see the houses, the kids. I remember, one day, we were talking with this American kid, maybe twelve years old and really tall. He meets this local kid about his age but half his size, and he saw where he lived and how little he had. The American was like, 'Is this real? How can this be part of the same world I live in?'"

Jackie (remember "Y'all need Jesus!"?) mentioned this same growth in the children, saying how, by the end of the week, they "really feel they came here for a purpose. They can feel open to hug the people, to deal with people. It's really amazing how people can change, how we human beings—even children—can feel empathy for people not like us at all."

All these perspectives make me think again about talents and gifts, how we all have the ability to help others, to build relationships and spread love. None of these accounts told of grandiose gestures or sophisticated actions like addressing large groups of people or performing magic tricks or even conducting long conversations in a foreign language. No. They involved playing with children, hugging them, treating them as equals, treating them with dignity, by using the gift of being human.

As the prayer time concluded, a few members of our team were culled to prepare the food for serving. The warm meals were ladled into multicolored plastic bowls with lids then stacked into boxes that the Charlotte kids carried into the church. While they were conveying the food across the field, we in the church were handing out more blue and pink bags of toys to the still-seated and remarkably well-behaved children. As the bowls of food arrived, we each grabbed a stack of bowls and handed one, along with a white plastic spoon, to each child. Each time we handed a bowl to a child, we said, "*Jesús te ama*" (Jesus loves you). I remember so clearly looking into a young boy's eyes as his hands reached for the bowl I held. He was careful not to overstretch and knock his trinket bag off his lap. As I looked at him and said, "*Jesús te ama*," I saw a slight widening of his dark eyes. We connected.

We now had a church-full of children, each with a bag of toys and a bowl of what I was told was the first food most would have had since at least the day before. But these kids continued to wait, not eating until the last person was served and a blessing was said; I didn't see one child sneak a bite. What patience. What respect. I cannot imagine a similar group back home under these circumstances behaving that well.

The interplay of food and religion was geared toward a broader community benefit as well. As Erling described it, "Many times, the parents never come to the church, but the kids do. So when we say to the kids, 'Jesus loves you. He sent this food for you,' they go home and tell their parents. So then the parents might come back later and say, 'Hey, my kid said that Jesus sent this food for him. Who is Jesus?' And that is how we start to open the door to Christ."

One passage from Livermore's book summed up how I felt after our half-day visit to *Iglesia Lirio de los Valles*: "Missions is at the very core of our calling. In my mind, missions isn't about getting souls saved. It's about living in light of our creation as image bearers of God. Missions—short-term, long-term, overseas, next-door—is about giving people a living picture of who God is, what God cares about, and how God acts."

I had not known it would happen, but we were in fact "image bearers" and gave each other "a living picture," a cool realization about talents and gifts standing in rural Central America in early January.

As we packed up and prepared to board the cage truck, a local teenage boy insisted on saying goodbye to me in English. I sensed my Spanish was probably stronger than his English, but it was clear he wanted to show this *gringo* that he had linguistic chops. We introduced ourselves, and he thanked me for coming. I then climbed the steel ladder into the truck bed, which was now almost empty of boxes—a nice reminder of the sustenance we had delivered. As we pulled onto the highway, the steady sway of the truck's suspension and medium-pitched din of the rugged tires on the concrete roadway lulled most of our Charlotte Christian charges to sleep. Observing their cat naps, Charles reflected on the experience they had just had: "Who knows how this experience might change their lives? Who knows in ten or twenty or thirty years, who of them are going to be doing spectacular things because of the experience they had here, the purpose of it all? I really think it will have a lifelong impact on these kids." What an impact, what a gift . . . one these kids both gave and received.

13

Volcanic Force

Talents and gifts come in all shapes and sizes—the bones and body parts of our collective existence. Part of the gifts we gave and received that morning at the church were relationship and connection. While interacting with other people is a normal human activity, doing so is in fact a talent; it is part of ministry. Very few of us will ever minister from a pulpit or address a congregation in a church. But we all can minister. For the majority of us, ministry occurs on a neighborhood street corner, in someone's home, in an office building, or on the phone or in front of a computer screen. When we are focused on others, sharing our talents and gifts and opening our humanity, we are in ministry. We are being an instrument of God's love and a vessel for God's grace. The labels might be daunting, but they fit.

I think about my own career and how the path I have led has revealed and honed the talents I was given and the ministry I perform. Leadership was something that seemed to show up early, as a football team captain, student body leader, fraternity president. It was in this last role that I learned the meaning of what leadership should be in my life. One day I was sitting in a fraternity brother's room complaining about how I felt like I always had to be the one to make decisions and wondering why someone else couldn't make the call every now and then (yes, I was whining). Of course our "decisions" then were pretty minor, at times sophomoric, as college social and residential life deliberations can be. But I was having a moment of feeling burdened.

Rather than empathize or try to explain away my sentiment, my friend sort of got in my face, with the whole finger-jabs-to-the-chest thing. He basically said, "Hey look, man. We're a big group, and in any group there are roles to play. Our group has guys who recruit new brothers, guys who set up parties, even guys who clean up late night. Each guy plays the role based on what he is best suited for. And since we are a group, someone has to be the leader. If it so happens that you are best suited to be our leader, then be our leader. Do your job."

As I look back on my friend's admonition, his words transformed how I saw the role of a leader. Being in charge is not about being the smartest or the most gifted or the one who talks the most. It's about identifying who is best suited to play that role and then about that person working with everyone to determine the needs and wants of the group and organizing resources to achieve an outcome. This view removes ego from the role of leader; it is simply another role that needs to be filled. Now that I have had the opportunity to lead in multiple contexts—business, nonprofit, faith, and family—I hope I use this it's-not-about-me-it's-about-the-group attitude as my prevailing perspective.

In addition to leadership, I believe I have a talent in communications (although you are the one reading this book, so you be the judge). I enjoy writing and public speaking, particularly distilling complex or disparate subject matter into reflections and speeches that are compelling and concise. Speaking of concise, I love Mark Twain's quip that "I would have written you a shorter letter, but I didn't have enough time."

Along with written and spoken communications, I find myself often in the role of group facilitator, which I suppose is a combination of being a leader and a communicator, listening to others and knowing when to encourage participation (especially from you introverts out there; we know the gears are turning even though your lips don't move much!) and how to keep a conversation headed in the right direction.

Facilitation is a component of a larger, more nebulous concept: change management, one of the wonkier terms of the business world. Change management, to me, is the process of guiding a group of people to a different way of interacting or toward a different set of goals, managing the change from where they are to some better future state. Change management has been a recurring theme along my life journey, particularly in my business career and leadership of a school board.

While the term may be more common in corporate speak, it applied well to our six days in Pochocuape. We were there—Samaritans International and Servants With a Heart—to improve people's lives, to change in some brief way the trajectory of their journeys, at least in a spiritual sense if not in a sustainable physical one. Managing this change required everyone involved to share their talents and gifts with each other and with the many Nicaraguans with whom we interacted.

After my experience in Nicaragua—specifically after the realization at the church about our being *actual* missionaries—it occurred to me that Jesus Christ was the greatest change manager in the history of the world. He came along at a time when polytheism was prevalent and many populations were ruled autocratically, with entrenched hierarchies imposing limited rights on stratified constituencies. These empires and kingdoms were typically ruled and expanded by bellicose means.

The origins of the Jewish faith, history's first sustained monotheist orthodoxy, offered a different approach, initiating more equality and recognizing more dignity for individuals. But it was Jesus, of course Jewish himself, who brought true societal transformation, espousing the notion that the poor shall become rich and the last shall become first. He recruited as disciples uneducated blue-collar types like fishermen and dock hands, as well as a tax collector—as despised as any vocation at the time. Jesus spent time with beggars, prostitutes, lepers—not the typical inner circle religious types. From his initial teachings and first twelve followers, however, a religion and an ethos have grown that, today, account for over two billion people's spiritual belief system, the largest religion in the world.

Our student-nap-inducing drive from the church community lasted about an hour and ended at *Parque Nacional Volcán Masaya* (Masaya Volcano National Park). I had never been to an active volcano, and the cage truck climb to the crater afforded a panoramic view of lava fields in all directions, where jagged but benign boulders and formations belied their original deadly, molten form. Small trees and occasional flowers jutted through the petrified landscape, providing sporadic color breaks in the monotone chocolate canvas, small signs of nature's perpetual renewal.

Our excitement grew as the twisting, turning road revealed occasional glimpses of volcanic steam escaping from the gaping mountaintop above, the truck's manual transmission whirring at high pitch as the heavy vehicle battled the incline. We arrived at a crater-side parking lot, where painted in every parking space was a giant white arrow pointing back down the road we had just come up. When I asked Patrick what the arrows were for, he said they were to ensure all vehicles could escape quickly should the volcano erupt. *Huh.*

As I climbed out of the truck, the air felt thick and moist, weighing down the hair on my forearms. My nose filled with a slight tinge of sulfur, which drew my gaze to the lazy plumes of steam burping slowly out of the crater. As we peered over the rim, several hundred feet wide, I could see a few faint dots of actual lava far below. As fascinating as this view was, my most memorable image from the visit was something I caught out of the corner of my eye: At the very top of the volcano, perhaps fifty feet above our perch and a hundred yards off, stood a giant cross, its vertical portion composed of three symmetrical tree trunks bound together and its horizontal cross of three shorter pieces of wood, one of which was askew. In the foreground of my visual field, standing at the far end of the parking lot, was one of our armed Samaritans guards, the outline of his handgun visible beneath his purple shirt.

I snapped a photo of the image, with the cross in the upper left corner of the frame and the guard in the lower right. Sharing this picture with people after the trip, I used the photo caption, "Watching over us from above and below." By the way, there was nothing threatening about this or virtually any spot we visited, but as I mentioned before, safety and precaution were of the highest priority.

As the grandeur of the crater sank in, Patrick pulled us together and informed us of the spiritual significance of active volcanoes in this part of the world. I had read about the prominence of spiritual warfare in Latin America, where certain portions of the population believed in Satan and in the region's pre-Christianity demonic influences. Patrick related how volcanoes were hotbeds (sorry, couldn't resist) of such ideologies, home bases for witch doctors and self-proclaimed sorcerers to promote their satanic doctrines as paths out of poverty and hunger.

While I do not believe in witchcraft in a pagan sense, I do believe in the influence of Satan on my life as a Christian. A keystone of Christianity—and of Judaism and Islam for that matter—is that God gave us free will, the ability to decide for ourselves what to do, how to act, and whether to choose good or evil. Adam and Eve's free will compelled them to ignore God's warning not to eat from the forbidden tree; they chose to do the wrong thing, committing the original sin. But it is widely known that the Bible says they were not alone when they ate the fruit; a snake was there as well, encouraging them. That snake was the manifestation—we Christians believe—of Satan, the fallen angel whose purpose is to oppose and undo the good that God compels in us.

In the first part of this book, I talked about the negative space of evil and the tethering weight of despair that challenge what is good and hopeful. These are Satan's lair, the realms he inhabits, tempting us to do wrong. The more aware I have become of my faith journey—an awakening this mission trip accelerated—the more conscious of the ugly lure of temptation I have become. Over the years I have given up pornography, overeating, and (most recently) foul language—to name three Satan-sanctioned activities I now resist, thanks to my relationship with God. The allure of consumption and the complacency of wealth that surround me in my normal life further compound the dangers of temptation, but these embarrassments of riches were conspicuous by their absence in Nicaragua. I recall Jeff saying how Satan did not have to work as hard in places like the United States because "materialism does his work for him," taking developed-world Christians' eyes off the what-would-Jesus-do ball.

Patrick spoke to these dark, satanic dynamics in Nicaragua, noting how doctrinal differences among the country's strands of Catholicism and Protestantism created space for malfeasance: "These dark leaders would provide a new set of rules and regulations, and they would play people against one another, particularly when different sets of Christians couldn't agree on everything. Using Satan, they realized how important Jesus dying on the cross is to Christians; you can't get into Heaven without the cross. Satan's not a dummy. He figured out that if he took away the cross, you might have thousands of believers who all of a sudden had no connection to Jesus. These bad people would exploit that, taking advantage of folks who already had nothing."

Samaritans International has a big challenge when they come upon a community where opposing forces—those who worship God and those who worship Satan—are in play. Patrick told us how the food can make all the difference: "In the work we do, you literally have whole communities that call out to Satan for their healing, for their food, for their supplies, everything they need. They call out to Satan as their god. When we bring in the food and teach that Jesus is the true God and Jesus provided the food, it completely conflicts what they've learned. They have never heard our story—God's story—and the food helps them believe because of what we stand for. One time we got like ten witch doctors to walk away from witchcraft. They said, 'We prayed for years to our god for food, and it never came. You guys came preaching Jesus and carried food, so, obviously, your God's stronger than ours, and we want to serve the strongest God.'"

Hearing this account, standing crater-side of an active volcano surrounded by miles of barren lava fields, with that giant cross towering above us, I felt the presence of God. The feeling was my next brush with *unvarnished faith*, whereby life seemed to be stripped down to the core elements of good and evil. The choices were so

dramatic—God or Satan—but so vital given the life-or-death impli-
cations of food and economic conditions surrounding us.

As we climbed into the truck and followed the giant white arrows
out of the parking lot, I sensed a lightening of both the air and the
mood as we rumbled away from an alleged spiritual battlefield.

14

To Whom Much
Was Given

The balance of Tuesday would be the only touristy segment of
the week, consisting of a boat ride around a portion of Lake
Nicaragua, a much larger—and less polluted—body of water
than Lake Managua (near Mateare). We then walked around the
lakeside city of Granada, a historic collection of Spanish-influenced
cathedrals and colonial landmarks. We dined in a cobblestoned alley
just off the main town square, with students at one table and adults
at another.

I chuckle recalling Jeff chiding Rone for "going soft" by schedul-
ing these sightseeing and leisure activities. Rone answered that such
a hiatus in the hard-core missionary routine helped promote positive group psyche and stateside parental calm, as well as provided an
appreciation for the broad cultural divides in the country, contrasting

downtown Granada with our trash dump and remote village experiences. I will say that the couple of hours of tourism were an odd change; I was enjoying being in mission mode, and the adjustment to tourist mode—which ironically had described much of my previous international travels—was underwhelming. But I suspect the respite was helpful for any of the kids who may have been further outside their comfort zones than they cared to be.

Time—how we spend the precious hours of each day—is the greatest gift any of us has to offer. In volunteer circles, people talk about giving the three Ts: time, talent, and treasure. Our talents are those collective bones and body parts I mentioned earlier. Our time, however, is limited, finite, constantly in demand. Perhaps unlike any talent we can share, giving someone the gift of time is unique; you have only one opportunity to give someone your time. We were all giving days of our time on this trip, spending hours in various villages and feeding centers, all the while dedicating minutes of interaction with local kids, local adults, and with each other. But it was the seconds—the eye contact, the quick smile, the touch on the shoulder, the strong hug—that were the most authentic, human, and dignifying gifts we exchanged.

Gray Keller is an author and philanthropist I have gotten to know over the past few years. In *Bless*, a short but punchy reflection on ways to dignify others through everyday acts, he writes, "Simply being with people in a special way can bless their lives in ways you might not realize. . . . You have a wealth of love and joy you can give to others through a warm smile, a gentle touch, or a timely word of encouragement."

These gifts cost us nothing but time, but they could be invaluable to their recipient, regardless of whether they are a small child in a Latin American churchyard, a coworker in a downtown office building, or a loved one in your family room.

The gift of time may have an even greater impact in the

communities where I live, with our luxuries and one-percenter "problems." What do you give the person who has everything? You give them time. You cook dinner for your parents. You call a friend just to ask how he is doing. You ask your spouse how her day was, and then you look her in the eye and listen, your phone in your pocket or the other room. These are gifts of self—the most intimate, customized, and priceless gifts there are.

Several years ago I stumbled upon the Bible passage Luke 12:48 (ESV), and it spoke to me more than any other scripture before or since. Luke writes that Jesus said, "Everyone to whom much was given, of him much will be required, and from him to whom they entrusted much, they will demand the more." I grew up in a safe neighborhood, went to a private school, then to a renowned college and graduate schools. I have lived in nice places. I have never truly had to worry about making my mortgage payment and rarely about where my next meal would come from (on those rare occasions when I did, it was usually due to lack of planning, not funds). So Jesus's instruction about the obligation to give back resonates deeply. I have this passage printed on the bottom of my computer monitor and reference it in just about every speech I give, even in secular environments.

On a lighter note, when I recently shared the importance of this passage with a college buddy, he quipped how his mother "pushed that philosophy on us our entire life. I never knew it as a Bible quote. I thought it was more from Spider-Man or something." Whether it came from a Marvel action hero or from the ultimate Christian action hero, this passage encourages me to give more than my fair share, in whatever context that applies.

Speaking directly to the third T, treasure, I am stirred by one of Jesus's proclamations regarding wealth. He is quoted in three of the Gospels saying that it is easier for a camel to go through the eye of a needle than for a rich person to enter the kingdom of God, continuing his insistence that those rich in earthly possessions will be poor in heavenly ones, that the "first shall be last." The pastor at my church addressed this concept in a homily a few years ago, saying he did not believe it was *having* wealth that would challenge one's likelihood of a bountiful afterlife, but what one *chooses to do* with wealth that would make the difference.

This idea of choice evokes another Bible passage: "If someone who has worldly means sees a brother in need and refuses him compassion, how can the love of God remain in him?" (1 John 3:17). I combine these wealth concepts—of much being given and required, of a camel and a needle eye, of choice and compassion— into an awareness of my place in society. I hope to live my life and share my blessings in ways that enrich the world both materially and spiritually.

Considering the concept of philanthropy, I also think about stewardship, which to me is not about leadership and the hierarchy it establishes but about caring for other people—or nature—by influencing and nurturing them positively. I look at wealth and financial assets in this way. What each of us has in terms of money, property, and other items of monetary value may technically be ours, but it is also the world's; we are merely stewarding them during our time here. I like the Native American proverb that says the earth was not given to us by our parents but loaned to us by our children.

I heard a speaker once talk about The Giving Pledge, a campaign founded by Bill Gates and Warren Buffett that asks extremely wealthy people to donate the majority of their assets to charity. Rick Warren has a cool way of looking at this idea of stewardship, equating how people should act during their brief stay on earth to how they might act if someone loaned them their beach house for a weekend: "They used it like it was theirs because they were told to, but they knew it didn't belong to them." Warren says we should carry "spiritual green cards" to remind us that our stay here is temporary; our true citizenship is in Heaven.

The practices of faith-based giving and stewardship are critical underpinnings of Servants With a Heart. During our trip Jeff touched on how his and Suzanne's faith journeys led to their acceptance of this calling: "I remember first *really* exploring the Bible in my late thirties and reading all these passages about servants and Jesus's comments about how the greatest among you will be a servant and just how much that impacted me.

"When Jesus is asked what are the greatest commandments, and he says, 'Love God, and love your neighbor,' He is saying we are all neighbors here in this world, on this planet. I remember asking myself, *Do you have the ability to sense a problem and do something about it, something for that person and take care of them?* Jesus talked about acting with a servant's heart. Over the years, the idea of a servant's heart has become immensely important to us."

Jeff and Suzanne describe acting with a servant's heart as using the lens of empathy to spot opportunities and then channeling a sense of compassion to make a difference. It became clear to me that my brother and sister-in-law had come up with the perfect name for their organization. I was proud to sport its logo on my T-shirts all week.

After our twilight dinner in Granada, we strolled the town square briefly but were ready to return to the compound, close to twelve hours after we left it on the way to *la iglesia* that morning. For the ride home, Jeff, Charles, and I climbed into the bed of the Hilux. Charles and I sat on a large Igloo cooler in the front below the roll bar, and Jeff plopped down on the remains of one of our SWH food boxes, its cardboard providing some cushioning.

The night was calm and mild, the kind of perfect temperature that causes you to feel neither heat nor cold. Given our distance from the big city of Managua, stars filled the sky, providing a serene, twinkly umbrella for our hour-plus trip. Along the way I had the chance to ask Charles about his family's company, a multigeneration printing business currently dealing with the opportunities and challenges of digitization and industry consolidation. As a fellow multigeneration family business owner, he patiently fielded my salvo of queries as we sped along.

The more I learned about Charles—how much he cared about his employees, how he shared decision-making with his brother even though Charles was in charge, and how he patiently worked through ownership issues with his father—the more I understood why Jeff was so fond of him. He had a huge heart—yes, a servant's heart. What a great friend to have. In fact, one of the things about my family of which I am most proud is the friends each of us has. When I think about the closest two or three friends of each of my brothers and my parents, a common trait is that each has a big heart.

Speaking with Charles on the drive also helped me refine a developing lens in my life, one to which I have not committed but continue to ponder: Is it possible that the world is composed of givers and takers? Does every person fall to one side or the other of an energy and attention transaction? I am not sure, but as I move through successive stages of life, I think maybe this is the case. There are of course degrees of giving and taking, a continuum along metaphorical and metaphysical axes, but I think everyone ultimately either gives or takes. Some people believe they are takers but are actually givers; they don't realize their generosity and maybe don't feel as worthy as they should. And sadly there are takers who believe they are givers, a cadre who might not see themselves and the world how they really are.

When we arrived back at *Embajada*, several of the students' weary expressions indicated they had dozed off on the long journey home.

I made a quick goodnight call to Kelly (just one hour ahead of me and far more of a night owl), during which I briefly updated her on our day, particularly about the realization from the morning that I was *actually* being a missionary; it was weird even saying the words aloud. We discussed how neither of us thought we would be able to be a conduit of God in such an explicit fashion. I guess being in relationship—as a vessel of God's love—was my purpose.

I hadn't begun to process what that meant. With hindsight, however, I appreciate that not all talents and gifts have to be developed or unique to be effective. That day I saw how God used me in ways I never imagined, an instrument helping others and making the world spin just a fraction truer on its moral axis.

Part 4

WEDNESDAY: SERENITY

"What day is it?" asked Pooh.
"It's today!" squeaked Piglet.
"My favorite day," said Pooh.

—A. A. MILNE, *Winnie-the-Pooh*

15

Jesus Bucket

I awoke Wednesday morning before my alarm, before dawn, before the rooster crow. My brain's overnight tollbooth operator ceded control to its daytime counterpart. Typically when I first awake, my mental awareness is faint, my thoughts ill formed or irretrievable. But today I was oddly aware of my mind matter: I should write another book, one about this trip. And I should start now.

The week before the mission I had published my first book, *Our Way*, a biography on my father. The 365-page tome stemmed from ninety-five interviews with my father, our family, and myriad coworkers, fellow volunteers, and friends, as well as from hundreds of correspondences, speeches, private letters, and my first-person account of our family and our family business. I was proud of the final product, particularly as evidence of my family's willingness and ability to share our story in a transparent and thoughtful way. And I learned to employ my bestowed literary talent. Thank you, God, and thank you, The Haverford School English Department. The fact that the book appeared on Amazon.com right before the trip was—so I believed at the time—a coincidence, a circumstance of timing and the random nature of life. I similarly (at the time) considered that morning's idea about a second book to be a product of my subconscious, a vague rumination conjured by my slumbering self.

As I have reflected on my fourth day of the mission, however, I have pivoted to the likelihood that coincidence and subconscious were not the best explanations for these seemingly unrelated events. I keep coming back to the concept of serenity: a calm awareness of what I can and cannot control and a recognition of the role God plays in the course of my life.

Speaking of bodily and mental reflections, goose bumps are one of those someone-a-lot-smarter-than-me-probably-understands oddities of the human body. We can get them when we are cold; I guess that makes sense, maybe the brain's way of alerting the skin. But why do we get them when certain emotions sweep us? And why does our throat lump or our eyes pool? There is likely a scientific or medical explanation involving hormones or pheromones or some kind of 'mones. Goose bumps were among life's mortal mysteries for me—until breakfast that morning, anyway. I ate across from my fellow tattoo artist, Dena, and told her about my early morning book idea. Hearing my words, she recoiled a bit and then held out her forearm, an array of faint blonde arm hairs standing upright. With wide-eyed enthusiasm she proclaimed, "Look! The Holy Spirit!"

What? Holy Spirit? Sure, I knew about the Holy Spirit, the third leg of Christianity's Trinity—Father, Son, and Holy Spirit. (By the way, I am relieved that many Christian denominations have substituted *Holy Spirit* for the more common term from my childhood, *Holy Ghost*, a reference I found visually terrifying.) Dena's point was that goose bumps, watering eyes, and lumpy throats may all be signs that the Holy Spirit is alive in you, a corporeal manifestation of the Lord. (Remember how I mentioned she wears her faith on her sleeve?) She said the idea of my writing a book about our mission resonated immediately with her and that I had to do it; the goose bumps, aka the Holy Spirit, told her so. I was on day four of the mission, immersed in Christianity and fixated on my faith walk, so why not? Goose bumps are the Holy Spirit! And maybe I will write that—ahem—*this* book?

The Reverend Frank Allen is the rector of St. David's Church, the largest Episcopal Church in Pennsylvania. He is a fellow Duke grad, a friend, and a mentor on my spiritual journey. In writing why God sent the Holy Spirit among his believers during the time of Pentecost (just after Jesus's final ascension to Heaven), Reverend Allen says it was "so that the entire world would know about the love, forgiveness, peace, and presence of God in their lives. When we are not quite sure what to do next and start to become filled with a sense of direction, that's the Spirit. When we are using some of the gifts God has given us and some amazing things start happening around us, that's the Spirit. And when we feel a deep sense of God's presence in our hearts, that's the Holy Spirit."

I like the idea that divine thread might connect certain events and circumstances in life, that there might be a higher influence over why things happen, whether it was Dena's goose bumps or my semi-conscious idea to write this book.

Little did I know I would acquire a second useful faith concept from my breakfast with Dena ("Breakfast with Dena" sounds like a country music song). But then she proceeded to tell me about *her* morning reflections. She was a veteran missionary, having made prior trips to Latin America and participated in several Christian outreach programs back in North Carolina, many through Mercy Matters, the ministry she founded and operates. She said that, earlier that morning, she had noticed how the first few days in Nicaragua had nourished her soul and filled her spiritually; she said the trip had filled her "Jesus bucket."

You know those metaphors that instantly make sense? They are so vivid and well-suited that no explanation is needed? *Jesus bucket* was such a term for me, how she meant that she had been spiritually enriched by the work we were doing and the people we were seeing. Having a full Jesus bucket made Dena—or any of us—a really good version of herself: "You crave your Jesus bucket being full. I mean, you come home from these trips, and you've had so much of the Holy Spirit poured into you. And now you've got this bucket, and it's sloshing over and you feel so great." *Sloshing*—I love it!

She continued, explaining how the bucket slowly empties and we regress to less desirable versions of ourselves. "These trips are in January, and by about March I'm like, 'Whoa, I need to go back. My bucket's getting empty.' I was about ready to punch somebody in the head today." She continued, "Or you know that guy who cuts you off on the road, forcing you to slam on the brakes, and now you want to pull back around him and hit your brakes to make *him* stop?" (Author's note: Dena is a sweetheart. I cannot imagine her contemplating hitting someone in the head. Maybe cutting someone off, okay, but haven't we all?)

With all this talk about the Holy Spirit, Jesus buckets, and road rage, I find myself fixated on the idea of control—what I can control and what I cannot—and therefore on the well-known twentieth-century meditation the Serenity Prayer: "God, grant me the serenity to accept the things I cannot change, the courage to change the things I can, and the wisdom to know the difference." Believed to be authored by Reinhold Niebuhr, this prayer is incorporated into myriad faiths and organizational doctrines, perhaps most famously Alcoholics Anonymous as a cornerstone of recovery.

I relate to this prayer in three ways, all of which have profound meaning for the events that transpired on Wednesday in Nicaragua and for where I am in life. The first is that there are no coincidences. The more I have grown in my faith, the more I believe things do not happen at random; even if I cannot control something, it does not mean it is not bound by the divine thread I mentioned earlier.

Second is the notion of being comfortable in my own skin, something I unknowingly struggled with for much of my adult life. A big part of serenity for me is learning to be at peace with who I am and where I am on my journey. I have the utmost respect for people who know exactly who they are and are at peace with it.

Finally is the idea of being present, of living in the moment, unburdened by what was or what may be. It is cliché but true: We cannot change the past. And our ability to impact the future, while certainly arguable, pales in comparison to our ability to throw our whole selves into the now and make this moment the best darn moment it can be.

After the not-your-typical-chit-chat breakfast with Dena, everyone mustered in the compound's chapel to hear a morning devotional from my brother Jeff. The title and theme of his remarks were—appropriately—"Servants with a Heart." It was inspiring to hear him elucidate the importance of this phrase, as well as learn a lot more about his faith journey.

To prepare us for the day ahead, Jeff challenged us not just to be the hands and feet of Jesus but to be the heart of Jesus as well, to have a servant's heart. He spoke movingly about why he invested in the business he runs, Jenkins Restorations, which restores homes and businesses after fire and flood damage. Jeff related a story about a Jenkins employee named Pip, who had comforted a young man whose father had just perished in a house fire. Jeff referenced a letter the young man had written to the company after meeting Pip: "Toward the end of the day of the fire, I was just sitting there in shock, waiting for the coroner to arrive. The firemen were going about their business, rolling hoses, etc. It was just me and my dad, his body in a body bag. I was very much in a state of shock.

"Pip came up, sat down next to me, and was talking to me—not about you guys or business or anything like that, just talking to me, doing his best to comfort me at the time. He didn't have to do it, and with all the chaos still going on, I'm sure he had a ton to do. I felt so very alone. But for that moment, talking with Pip, I felt I just might get through it all.

"Don't tell Pip I said this (I think he'd be embarrassed by it), but it really made a difference."

Sad but inspiring. Jeff pointed out how Pip was acting with a servant's heart, a phrase that now appears in Jenkins's mission statement: "Restoring property and lives with a servant's heart." And sorry, Pip, but a bunch more people now know your story.

Jeff then explained his ethos in a way that our group, particularly the students, could grasp: "I think of a servant's heart as something that's always being proactive to help others. It's the empathy that allows you to sense the struggle somebody is going through. And it's the compassion to do something about it: when somebody assists the elderly or the person you see at the airport that sees somebody drop something and responds right away to pick it up for them."

Feeling empathy, expressing compassion, and being in action— sounds like a pretty good way to live, again that whole Christianity as a contact sport thing I mentioned earlier. Jeff referenced important verses from the Bible, particularly the parable of the Good Samaritan and Jesus's Beatitudes from the Sermon on the Mount, which helped cast his spiritual foundation. He talked about growing up in a privileged home, raising his family in a privileged area, and about how the majority of people living in the United States were privileged compared to many other people the world over. His reflections were prescient, given the emphasis on privilege these days. Jeff concluded his remarks in the same place he started:

"Let's talk about heart. You think about heart. You think about life. You think about the pumping of blood. It's what allows us to live. You also think about heart on an athletic field. It's guts. It's having the big heart to be able to do something beyond what you think your body can do. We've got Proverbs 3:5 that says, 'Trust in the Lord with all your heart, and lean not on your understanding.' When I read this verse, I think of the popular saying, *I'm all in*. You know? If you have heart, you're all in. You're all in on this thing."

The energy in the room was high when Jeff finished; I know my high school sports muscle memory was activated for sure. It was no coincidence Jeff delivered that devotional on that morning with what lay ahead. *Bravo, brother!*

16

No Coincidences

The week's outreach efforts had so far brought us to a trash dump, a bleak mountaintop village, and an impoverished community church—all appropriately austere missionary milieus. When I heard today's outing would take us to a seaside resort community, I will admit to being bewildered but excited; images of placid surf, steel drums, and beachside gazebos filled my mental moviemaker. We packed up, snapped the proof of life, and loaded into the cage truck for the hour-plus commute to a tourist town along the Pacific Ocean.

Rone, who during his military career in special operations had specialized in counterinsurgency, relayed something that struck me, the latest in a now-long list of things I was learning on this trip: Just because we were going to a resort community, do not think the people to whom we will minister will be well off. He said the community that day, while bordering the Pacific Ocean, would be just as impoverished, its people just as in need, as the others we had seen that week. Okay, mental images gone, curiosity piqued.

After descending Pochocuape's hillside, we had to cross through a small commercial section of Managua. As we all stood in the flatbed cage and motored along a busy four-lane road, the truck suddenly hitched, then lurched forward, testing our urban surfing abilities. The truck was breaking down, and our driver, Morgan, muscled the weighty, crippled vehicle to the curb. The Samaritans guides inspected the engine, concluded that the repair would not be a quick one, and radioed back to the compound for alternate transportation. Fortunately, given the logistics expertise of folks like Erling and Jimmy, a bus was soon on its way.

The breakdown occurred in a populated area—the only portion of the long commute with anything but open fields dotted by small, sporadic rural communities. The small strip mall next to where we stopped happened to have, of all things for a group of high schoolers on a hot morning, an ice cream parlor. Bonus! Rone made the quick—and, let's face it, easy—decision to usher everyone into the air-conditioned store and pay for a round of midmorning treats, the *exact* kind of reason one carries petty cash.

So our truck had broken down and our mission was now off schedule. But, as Charles quickly observed, we were marooned not in the middle of nowhere but in a populated, commercial neighborhood. We were close enough to the compound that a bus would be there shortly. And—trumpet blaring and lights piercing the gloom— an ice cream shop had just begun its business hours. Charles noted how what could have been a total nightmare ended up being barely a blip, with the added bonus of dessert in the morning. One of our students remarked similarly, impressing us adults with his recognition of what we can control and what we cannot and the faith to accept how events take place in our lives.

Were the timing and location of our mechanical mishap coincidences? Maybe. Perhaps it seems too dramatic to attribute them to divine intervention. Maybe. But maybe not. Pope John Paul II said, "God's hand was always at work, and there was no such thing as coincidence." James Redfield writes in *The Celestine Prophecy* that the first insight toward spiritual awareness occurs "when we become conscious of the coincidences in our lives, [that] mysterious movement is real and that it means something . . . the feeling that some other process is operating." So maybe there are in fact *no* coincidences? In the time since that first trip to Nicaragua, I have become more and more convinced of this construct, a combination of subsequent life events and an increasingly deliberate faith journey compelling me to this interpretation—and serene acceptance—of the sequencing of my time on earth.

The concept of the faith journey, and, more broadly, of faith itself, are difficult to grasp or explain. I describe faith as an acknowledgment of what is unprovable but helps guide our lives and bring meaning to our existence. The book of Hebrews says that "Faith is the realization of what is hoped for and evidence of things not seen." Faith explains life beyond what science, circumstance, and the oh-well-shrug-your-shoulders concept of luck can.

Regarding science—and the related concept of logic—I have taken several profile tests in my career that gauge left brain versus right brain dominance and have always come out somewhere in the middle, possessing approximately equal influences of the more logical, organized left brain and the more creative, artsy right brain. Given my logical side, I struggled for a long time with the idea of faith and certain events and circumstances being something other than scientifically or factually explainable—or simply random or coincidental. My control freak persona was ill at ease.

I have learned, however, that I can only get so far with logic, with the observable and the explainable. At some point, I arrive at an impasse where what has happened or what could happen leaves a gap in explanation or expectation. Faith allows me to find comfort—serenity—with uncertainty. This is part of the mystery of faith. God created us in God's image, but we are incapable in human form of grasping the whole-being-ness that is God. There are things in this life that are beyond our comprehension. Faith is the vehicle that transports me through this mysterious journey.

My pastor suggested that, when I read the Bible, I parse certain stories' *scientific or historical facts* from their *biblical truths*. For example, many key figures in the Old Testament were said to have lived for hundreds of years, perhaps the oldest being Methuselah, who died at 969 years old. Scientifically, I do not believe that people could live that long, particularly thousands of years ago. But from a faith perspective—discerning the biblical truth—I accept that these people lived long lives during which they accomplished many meaningful acts.

In addition to our truck breaking down that morning in a safe, convenient location, a recent sequence of faith-related events at home helped cement my no-coincidences credence. I participate in three different fellowship groups, where small numbers of Christian men gather early in the morning to talk about the Bible and how it impacts our lives. Typically a handful to a dozen or more people participate, but on the rare occasion when attendance is lighter, we are still emboldened by Jesus's teaching: "For where two or three are gathered together in my name, there am I in the midst of them" (Matthew 18:20).

What I most appreciate about these groups is the parallel efforts of discerning the context and purpose of the biblical stories along with—perhaps more importantly—relating how those verses and events apply to our lives. One of the groups meets during the summer on the back porch of our Jersey Shore house. A couple particularly special moments with this group have been when I have had my Episcopalian father (in his eighties) seated on one side and my young adult Catholic son on the other.

It was a sequence of events involving the back porch group that convinced me of life's lack of coincidence. There is a key story from early in Jesus's ministry when He recruits His first disciples, fishermen from the Sea of Galilee. After the men return from a long, unsuccessful voyage, Jesus hops in one of the boats and instructs the men to cast their nets out deep, to which they immediately comply, despite their exhaustion and frustration. I find it fascinating that these guys were professional fishermen, weary from an all-night fishing excursion on which they got skunked, and here was this unknown carpenter telling them where to fish.

They follow His direction and soon fill their boats with a record haul, called "The Miraculous Catch." Upon returning to shore, Jesus informs the men they will no longer be fishermen but fishers *of* men, a cool play on words to explain their new role as evangelists. The men abandon their spoils on the shoreline, leave their lives behind, and set out with Jesus to form the initial band of disciples.

I think the reason I enjoy this story so much is that I love fishing and I love following Jesus—although I am pretty amateurish with both. Anyway, I decided I wanted a large print of "The Miraculous Catch" to hang in our Shore house. After an unsuccessful internet search, I paid a visit to Gary, a fellow participant in the Shore fellowship, who is a professional sculptor and owns an art gallery on the island that routinely displays Christian artwork. He is a lifelong Catholic (affectionately known as a "cradle Catholic"), with a deep belief in God, attending daily Mass and living his faith personally and professionally.

Visiting Gary proved to be a good idea and a bad idea. It was good because he had a viable suggestion, but it was bad—or at least naive on my part—as his suggestion was not to buy a (mass-produced, inexpensive) print from the internet or an art store but to commission a professional artist to create a (much more expensive) painting of the scene. Well, Gary does own an art gallery, and he does make his living selling and brokering professional artwork, so I should have known. Kelly and I own a handful of paintings from friends who were budding artists at the time of purchase but had never commissioned anything significant from a full-time professional. After several weeks of contemplation and procrastination, I agreed to proceed, establishing a budget and researching and interviewing Gary's suggested artist.

It was at this point in the story that the "coincidences" began. Late one sunny midsummer Friday afternoon, I went to the gallery to drop off the deposit for "The Miraculous Catch." While I was there, Gary told me about an interview he had done recently for a Christian podcast concerning a bizarre sequence of events involving a bronze statue he was producing for a church; the theme of the podcast was, fittingly, that there are no coincidences. The next morning Gary arrived for our fellowship meeting a few minutes early with an exhilarated look on his face. He sprinted up my porch steps with his iPhone in his hand. I asked him what was up, and he rattled off almost indecipherably that his podcast interview had just been released. *Okay, good for you, buddy.* But his animation seemed a bit over the top. He then thrust his smartphone into my face and told me to look at what the podcast host had titled the episode— one that had nothing to do with fishing or Jesus or disciples: "The Miraculous Catch."

Fast-forward a few months to Thanksgiving weekend. The artist had completed the piece and would drive to the Shore to hang it in our home, with Gary's assistance. As I awoke on the morning of the delivery and launched one of my Bible apps to read a morning devotional, I looked up what that day's prescribed Gospel reading was.

Keep in mind there are four Gospels, ranging in length from sixteen to twenty-eight chapters, and each chapter contains dozens of verses, meaning there are thousands of possible passages that could be assigned to any of the 365 days in a year. But on this particular day, the day my painting would be delivered, the assigned reading was from the beginning of Luke, chapter 5, dubbed "Jesus Calls the First Disciples." The mind blower, however, is that the other title of this passage is—yup, you guessed it—"The Miraculous Catch."

Later that morning, Gary texted me after making the same discovery, another reason to be—as someone once told me—"no longer surprised but always in awe." I realize that, in the grand scheme of things, events centering on a custom piece of art is a quintessential first-world story, and I am blessed to have the resources and network to beautify our home and honor our Maker in this fashion. Nonetheless, it convinced me once and for all that there are, in fact, no coincidences. Oh, and the painting looks awesome!

A final footnote on this story: During that same summer, Kelly and I purchased a small business that she now manages. The footnote involves Jesus's word play I mentioned above: fishermen to fishers of men. A friend of mine pointed out that the name of the business further cemented that there are no coincidences: "Go Fish."

17

Comfortable in
My Own Skin

Every day, I feel more aware of what I can control and what I cannot; it is no shocker there is a *ton* more in the latter category. My faith propels me along this path of awareness, my belief that God is all knowing and all powerful, that the plan for my life is unfolding as God wills it. Since Christians believe, however, that we were given free will, God's plans coexist with our decision-making and actions, as well as our temptations and whims. I do not know enough to know about how God's will and our free will interact. Are they more like a chemical suspension that mixes but never combines or more like acrylic paint colors that come together to transform into something permanently different? This question is one of many ponderings I have on my faith journey.

The Hindu concept of *karma* relates to the idea of control as well. Karma describes the effects your actions have, actions that will determine the form and quality of your next reincarnated life; this cycle of life–death–rebirth is called *samsara*. The better someone lives this life—controlling their actions—so believe Hindus, the better their stature will be in the next life, echoing the idea that there may be a connection to how well we assimilate our actions to what is good.

The cage truck breakdown proved to be almost a nonevent, versus the calamity it could have been had it happened in the countryside or had a tire blown out or, or, or. By the time we finished our ice cream (I went with mint chocolate chip with whipped cream—delish!), the passenger van and Hilux had arrived. Jeff, Charles, and I climbed into the now familiar cargo bed of the latter and led the small caravan back onto the road and westward out of town toward the coast. The scenery quickly turned rural, and we passed the occasional three-wheeled motorized cart or run-down horse-drawn trailer piled high with dried crops, farm tools, and miscellaneous equipment.

At one point I spotted ahead a flurry of dark shapes moving wildly along the shoulder of the narrow, paved two-lane road. As we sped closer, the swirl became a trio of giant wing-flapping buzzards homed in on the inside-out carcass of a dead dog splayed across the mouth of a rusty culvert at a bend in the roadway. Passing this graphic but understandable link in nature's food chain, my senses were further funked by the primordial squawks emitting from the birds' blood-soaked beaks.

The buzzard feeding frenzy, while a real-time example of things beyond our control, was only the second-most disturbing element of the ride. My cursing was number one. I had always cursed, but I think I convinced myself that I usually had the awareness and decorum to do so only in places I deemed "appropriate" (e.g., not around children, not in professional or public settings). Like many people, I probably started out as a teenager thinking cursing was cool, a rite of adulthood that I was earning with age. As an adult, I continued to curse. For some reason, on that morning journey in the back of a pickup truck in the western countryside of Nicaragua with Jeff and Charles, I felt compelled to amplify just about every other sentence with curse words.

With the benefit of hindsight, I realize that my foul language was a sign of disquiet, an uncertainty about who I was. I was not comfortable in my own skin. And there is no serenity if you are not comfortable in your own skin, with who you were meant to be and with your position and lot in life. As I have started to share with people over the past few years, this realization that I had become ill at ease with who I was, their initial reactions—most notably my siblings'—were more surprise than agreement. I had always been pretty successful in life and pretty confident (at times as a young professional, cocky) with who I was.

What I have discovered in recent years—fueled by an increased focus on my faith journey—is that much of my behavior had become about predicting how others would expect me to be and then assuming a façade to fill that persona. My bride dubbed this my need to "put on perfect." I realized that, over many years, I had created these suppositions of what others thought I should be, and I had become more and more anxious about playing those parts.

My motive was, in part, to make others comfortable. I have always considered myself a bit of a chameleon. We all do this to varying extents; it is polite and honors others' dignity. But where is the divide between being genuine and pandering? Where do the colors blur between accommodating another's personality and remaining true to your own? What behavior displays empathy versus insecurity?

It can be a fine line, and the line varies for each of us and for each situation. In Nicaragua, I sometimes got into dilemmas conversing with the locals. My Spanish still sounded pretty genuine from my schooling and experience living in Madrid, but my comprehension and vocabulary had become shadows of their former Spanish-major selves. As a result, a Nicaraguan would hear me say something with a decent accent, assume I *really* knew the language, and rattle off a fast, long response, of which I would often struggle to get the gist. It was not always natural for me to ask them to slow down—not to put on perfect.

Eventually I was able to connect my being uncomfortable in my own skin with anxiety. Anxiety is tough. I have it. We all do, in one form or another. I appreciate how debilitating it can be for many. Along with my anxiety about "putting on perfect," I battle with something that on the surface may not seem like a big deal, but for me and for my family, it can be damaging: my fear of being late. I struggle with showing up past when I say I will, pretty much concluding that if I am not on time, not only am I a horrible person, but civilization as we know it may end. Waaay out of proportion.

Don't get me wrong; I believe being on time is important and respectful and an expression of good character. But there is a huge divide for me between being *on time* and being *late*; sadly there have been times when my or my family's being late has caused me to become a really ugly version of myself, far from comfortable in my own skin.

The lack of epidermal ease used to manifest itself in insidious ways (like incessant cursing in the bed of a pickup), or as defensiveness (another of my strong suits), or—worse—anger (like when the family was running late). Losing one's temper is almost never good. The Bible says we should be slow to anger, justifying rage only in instances when God's will is not being followed, like if a person who cannot defend themselves is unfairly persecuted by someone with more power or resources.

Regrettably, my temper flares—mostly yelling, slamming a door, not listening to reason, but never hurting someone or one of our pets—have typically stemmed from events nowhere near as noble or deity-ordained: running late for a summer wedding, a contractor ringing the doorbell earlier than his dispatch said he would arrive, or being upset with my father and taking it out on Kelly by yelling at her when she was just trying to help me cope. I think you can guess none of these are hypotheticals; they all happened, a few examples of me blowing my top.

My epiphany was that in those moments, who I was being was someone not comfortable in his skin, questioning where I was in my journey. My six days in Pochocuape were a key entry into the realization log that I was not happy with who I was and where I was in life. Writing this book helped me immeasurably with being comfortable and recognizing what I can and cannot control. But I still have a long way to go.

Returning to my cursing in the back of the pickup, most faiths—and many people—would agree that cursing and anger are not the best expressions of ourselves. As a Christian, I see them both as failures, like I mentioned earlier, to be who Jesus would be if He were me. Anger is often a front for some deeper emotion—perhaps shame or insecurity or defensiveness—triggered like pushing the play button on an old tape deck with the same cassette queued to the same tired song.

While I am still working on my temper, I have made big strides with my cursing; shortly after this mission, I vowed to stop, cold turkey. Yup. I made the decision one day after reading yet another (I count at least four) admonition in the New Testament not to use foul language. It was from Paul's letter to the Colossians: "But now you must put them all away: anger, fury, malice, slander, and obscene language out of your mouths. Stop lying to one another, since you have taken off the old self with its practices and have put on the new self, which is being renewed, for knowledge, in the image of its creator"

(3:8–10). I like how these verses castigate other members of my vice club like anger and fury as well.

I read the passage and committed to stop cursing there and then. *How am I doing?* Okay, I think. I slip up once or twice a week, often to myself—a far cry from my previous profanity production. I also have to acknowledge my brother Jeff on this topic. He had committed to curbing his cursing years earlier but exhibited grace on that morning Hilux ride; he did not correct me or express unease at my language. I think he knew if I ever came to the point of questioning my language, I would have to get there on my own.

We all know people who are comfortable in their skin. I always think about one person who knows who he is and goes through life with the quiet ease that this understanding brings (he's super humble, so I won't out him). His steady demeanor personifies the adage, "still waters run deep." As our journey wound down and we approached the still waters of the Pacific, we were about to experience the comfort—and loving bonds—that living a life of faith provides.

18

Fellowship on the Sand

Nicaragua, like other Central American countries, has beautiful luxury resorts along the Pacific Ocean that international travelers frequent for surfing, fishing, fine dining, and high-end accommodations. The community we visited, where Samaritans International visits periodically, was not such a place. While it was touristy, with bright multicolored banners across the access road and what appeared to be, behind cement walls and dense foliage, attractive hotels, this vacation destination seemed to cater to a domestic or at best regional clientele.

We drove past the resorts and terminated our long commute in a parking lot along the beach. The sun was high in the sky, another hot day upon us. But the proximity of the ocean and the slight onshore breeze ensured that any rainforest-fueled humidity would be held at bay to the east, creating downright pleasant conditions. The beach was perhaps a hundred yards wide, the gentle rollers of the Pacific immediately visible, their rhythmic, drum-like crashing pleasing to my ears.

No sooner did we pile out of the vehicles and move into a large, thatch-roofed area at the beginning of the beach than locals (not tourists) started materializing: dozens of children out of the proverbial woodwork; a handful of men on horseback riding casually but purposefully up the beach toward us; and—most memorably—a half dozen or so older women donned in wrap skirts and aprons, their necks and arms draped with dozens of necklaces and bracelets, shuffling into the shaded area, ready to peddle their wares to us gringos.

I willingly shelled out twenty American dollars for two necklaces and a bracelet from one of the jewelry salesforce. I still wear the bracelet today; it helps keep me grounded and often brings warm memories to the fore. Because Samaritans visited this location regularly, Patrick knew the local pastor and alerted her we were coming. Presumably she had notified members of her community. They seemed to know the drill for when American missionaries show up.

We settled into a row of picnic tables at one end of the covered area—which was perhaps fifty feet by thirty feet, with large wooden columns throughout holding up the roof—to make crafts with the kids, my first time on bracelet making. During these interactions I discovered portrait mode on my iPhone and could now capture far more of the character and beauty of both the children and elderly women. I do not know if any of my photo subjects owned cell phones, but I was struck by the casualness with which I possessed my $800 phone in their company. Perhaps they were more used to seeing people like me—with my US creature comforts—than, say, the inhabitants of the trash dump may have been. My highlight of this time frame was meeting a ten-year-old rail-thin but handsome boy named Angel and throwing a Frisbee with him on the beach. Cute kid, universal connection.

While we crafted and played, a few of the Samaritans staffers set up the mobile propane stove in a corner of the covered space. We then relayed boxes of food from the vehicles to the pop-up kitchen, as well as to the edge of the building, where the horsemen were queuing, ready to return home with rice-and-soy sustenance. I had the chance to see the cooking process from the beginning, helping add the bags of food to the quickly simmering water. Food can add texture to any setting, a well-balanced meal providing nutrients but also conveying respect and honor to the recipients. Stirring the giant wok of SWH food, I was moved by this recognition of the dual physical and emotional nourishment we were preparing.

As the meals simmered to life, the Americans and Nicaraguans gathered together in the middle of the shaded area, which had become our church for the day. Jackie from Samaritans assembled everyone together using a portable microphone system and said a prayer, during which the local kids—despite the excitement of playing with the T-shirt-clad Americans (today's color was turquoise) and the anticipation of a warm meal—sat still, with eyes forward and full attention. I again reflected on how well-behaved Nicaraguan children were. I noticed a couple local girls, no older than our teenagers, holding babies, one of them off to the side, nursing her infant.

One of our J-termers gave her testimony, a story about a tragic loss from childhood. Her account was honest and raw and super sad. She commented how she "had left God" until about a year ago but now was more committed than ever to her faith, culminating in her decision to come on the trip. Once more I was moved to tears. Glances right and left revealed I was not alone.

While we chaperones struggled to compose ourselves (reminding me of Rone's "crack the shell" metaphor), the petition for prayers was made, when, like yesterday, the local children were asked to stand up if they wanted one of the missionaries to pray for them. Today was Wednesday, our third day in the field, so we had the routine down; there were few pauses before folks engaged with their Latin American sisters and brothers in Christ.

In between my own iterations of laying on of hands and praying over people (remember the terminology?), I observed one of our teenage boys approach a pint-sized kid standing by himself. Our guy dropped to one knee to establish eye contact, then placed his hands on the toddler's shoulders, bowed his head, and began to pray. The distance between us was too great and the din beneath the thatched roof too high for me to hear what he said, but I knew our boy didn't know much Spanish and was pretty sure the local kid knew no English, so nothing comprehensible was exchanged. I could tell the intercession was over when the J-termer pulled the boy in for a full-arm hug.

I expected the embrace to be brief, like that cursory squeeze you might see between basketball players before a game when their names are announced and they trot to midcourt. But, here on the cool sand, the two young boys held tight to each other, the little one's outstretched arms reaching up from his maroon tank top over the teenager's bony shoulders and around his sweat-soaked neck. They held each other for several beats, but it felt even longer. When they finally pulled apart, arms extended but hands remaining on each other, both had glistening streaks on their cheeks.

I still see those two boys crying in my mind now as clearly as if I were back in the midday shade of that large shelter near the Pacific Ocean. In homage to Dena's spiritual lesson from breakfast that morning, if this display of emotion from two geographically, culturally, and linguistically distinct children was not the Holy Spirit at work, then nothing is.

I relayed this event to Patrick later in the day. He said when you see something like that happen, you have to believe in the power of short-term mission trips. "You're out of your comfort zone," he said. "You're here. You don't really know everything that's going on, and then we start telling you, 'God's brought you to this point, allowed you to go on this trip, and wants to use you.' Then, all of a sudden, you pray for this person, you see them begin to cry, and you know that God's doing something in their heart and in their life, and you get touched, too. Your faith truly gets accelerated." *True that, Patrick. True that.*

After worship and prayers, we distributed the food: warm prepared bowls to the kiddos and full unopened boxes to the horsemen; they expertly strapped the cardboard cubes onto the horses, mounted their bare backs, and headed down the beach—literally riding off into the setting sun. Because I had awoken that morning with the idea to write this book, I had brought my audio recorder from the compound and now retrieved it out of my cargo shorts. I was going to interview the local pastor, the shepherd tending her flock, a metaphor that seemed more apt and more graspable in that agrarian, underindustrialized country than it does at my or perhaps any other church back in the States.

She and I came together so I could ask her a series of questions about the community and the impact missionaries had. Erling translated my queries (I didn't have *that* much faith in my Spanish and wanted to extract every insightful syllable). Like others had, she echoed the relationship between the food and the Word.

"Most of the people here in the community," she said, "they're not believers. But through the food, we can come, we can bring the kids here, and through the work, we can teach them who Christ is and what He did for us. Then they can come to Christ. When we say that we're going to cook, as we're cooking, you have the time to teach the Word. It's good because we have the food, and we also have the Word of God at the same time."

She also underscored the impact kids have on each other. "Our kids can see how the American children show the love of God through everything they bring. [The Americans] leave their houses, and they come all the way here just to share the Gospel with the kids. It's important."

I have learned through raising my own children, watching them play with their older cousins or interact with babysitters, how special the connections can be among young people as opposed to those between children and adults. I think the proximity of age creates bonds that intergeneration relations cannot. The idea that our team of missionaries was harnessing this youthful dynamic was a gift for all involved.

Shortly before we left—after getting one of our supply trucks unstuck from the soft sand—one of the jewelry peddlers from the morning approached Jeff and me as we were climbing into the Hilux. She carried a shallow round wicker basket covered with a pale green towel. While she did not speak, she smiled at us warmly, extended the basket, and pulled back the corner of the fabric, revealing a cluster of small rectangular pieces of bread, their crested tops yellowish orange. The sugary smell was terrific.

She extended the basket and moved her eyes from it to our mouths, indicating we should each take a piece, which we did. I took a bite; it was still warm and had a subtle sweetness to it—yum! We thanked her with a series of awkward nonverbal expressions—small bows, toothy grins, and a quick hug—and climbed into the truck. For some reason I did not want to eat the entire roll so looked around for a place to pitch the rest. Jeff sternly directed me otherwise: "You have to eat the whole thing!" Oh, right. One of the locals just gave *us* food. Of course I had to finish it; there was no way I could waste food! The irony was now apparent, as was—even more so—the kindness of her gesture, that she presumably went home to bake bread and likely hurried back to the beach to give it to us before we left.

She was using her talents, honoring our dignity, and exhibiting strong character. I think about how I almost took for granted how this small act of fellowship from this elderly woman, whose name I never got and whom I will almost certainly never see again, encapsulated the current dynamics and takeaways from our week—and summarized the themes of this book so far.

Reflecting on the beauty of the day—the seaside scenery, yes, but more so the faith-filled connections and kindness—I think about how much of Jesus's earthly ministry took place alongside and on the water. The miraculous catch, calming stormy seas, cooking breakfast for the disciples, and of course, walking on water. These are some of the most celebrated moments of Christianity, and none took place inside a church. What is it about where the land meets the sea that is so conducive to spiritual events? I think this is why I am so drawn to coastal areas, where humans, nature, and God come together and the universal bonds of creation and coexistence are on display.

19

Unwrapping Presence

What stuck with me most about the seaside woman giving me the gift of bread (yup, *that* symbolism works here) was how present she was. She seemed to know why we had come and that she could, in that moment, express her gratitude. The idea of being present, of focusing on the now, is the final aspect of serenity for me; it is something with which I have struggled for much of my life.

As I grew older and piled on more and more layers of adultness, I found myself less and less able to engage in what was happening in the moment, instead too often replaying events from the meeting at work or the conversation at home or overplanning the next meeting or conversation. When I am in the moment—any moment—adulting can make it hard to be present, making it feel like I am not as productive as I should be. I continue to work on focusing on the person, place, or thing right in front of me, of knowing that that practice is all the productivity I need.

Several years ago I was driving in our old neighborhood and came to a stop sign. As .the car slowed, I glanced ahead to the next block at an elderly couple walking arm in arm on the sidewalk. For some reason—and with no car behind me—I sat and watched. They came to the intersection and paused, not to look both ways before crossing but so the woman could bend down to a bush. The man did likewise. They then straightened up, looked both ways, and shuffled across the street, arms still interlocked. It was only after they had passed that I noticed the target of their attention: a rosebush. Yes, ladies and gentlemen, two people had just stopped to smell the roses. Now *that* is being present.

That floral flashback, however, is not my only memory of the importance of being present. Another has to do with toothpicks. Almost two decades ago, Kelly and I had two young children, the oldest of which was in his first year of preschool. One snowy winter day, I was working from home (a rarity back then), leading an all-day conference call with my team, who were all over the country and unable to commute to Philadelphia. This was during the time when multiperson (voice only) conference calls were coming into vogue, before you could video conference or share your screen. I was holed up in the spare bedroom in the back corner of the second floor, as far away as possible from the perpetual melee and clatter that define home life with young'uns.

Several wearying hours into the call, my son arrived home from preschool (it was half day and ended before the storm got bad). He sprinted up the stairs and barged through the closed-but-regretta-bly-not-locked door of my temporary office. I was vaguely aware of his hand in front of him holding something. But I was on my call, being important. So I raised my own hand and flexed it into the universal sign for *Halt!* Then physics took over, and the unstoppable force of his forward enthusiasm hit the immovable object of my I'm-busy-get-out stop sign.

Boom!

I immediately stopped talking and turned to see what had happened. Well, that vague "something" he had held in his hand had been a kiln-fired disk of clay, painted all the colors of the rainbow and holding some two dozen toothpicks standing in formation like a pint-sized forest. It had collided with the palm of my bossy hand. The creation was the first arts and crafts project I had ever received as a parent, and it now lay in pieces on the yellow shag carpet next to my chair.

My eyes panned up from the rubble to my son's face. His expression changed from pure joy to wide-eyed terror. I can only imagine the days of anticipation as he crafted it and waited for it to cure, the hours of excitement as he knew he was bringing it home, and the final seconds of euphoria as he learned that I was *actually* home as he sprinted through the back door, up the steps, and into the room. The poor kid.

That episode happened almost twenty years ago, and I still feel like such a jerk writing about it now. Needless to say, I was not able to shift my presence to what mattered in the moment. What I thought mattered didn't (and most of my colleagues had children and would have understood if I had dropped off briefly). What *did* matter was now a pile of matter strewn across the rug. Today that heap of jagged painted clay and jumbled toothpicks sits in a Ziploc on my office shelf—a reminder about what really matters.

And, son, since I haven't said this in a few years, I'm sorry I broke your masterpiece.

Serving the seaside children warm food and telling them *"Jesús te ama,"* observing a prayer between two intercontinental youths that led to tears, receiving fresh-baked bread from someone with rudimentary resources—these were all opportunities to be present, to focus on the now. I admit it was much easier to be in the moment given where I was, as opposed to where I usually am—in the United States, bound by technology and creature comforts, always a click away from revisiting yesterday or crystal-balling tomorrow. But I have gotten better. The more I use the repopularized acronym WWJD—what would Jesus do?—as my primary lens to approach each day, the more I have been able to home in on my current task or current conversation or current person in front of me, despite the ever-present and sinister siren call of my iPhone, tempting me to push the tiller of my focus toward the invisible but craggy rocks of distraction.

Mindfulness is largely about this idea of blocking out distraction and focusing on the present. Mindfulness is also what Vietnamese monk and Nobel Prize nominee Thich Nhat Hanh calls, "the substance of Buddhism":

> In Buddhism, our effort is to practice mindfulness in each moment—to know what is going on within and all around us. . . . Most of the time, we are lost in the past or carried away by future projects and concerns. When we are mindful, touching deeply the present moment, we see and listen deeply. . . . The most precious gift we can offer others is our presence.

This quote reminds me of what my mom would often write at the bottom of invitations for parties she and my dad would host: "Your presence is the only present we want." So, just like every other theme in this book, serenity—what you can control versus what you cannot, being comfortable in your skin, being present—is central to myriad spiritual practices and human interactions, reinforcing the universal importance of cherishing our relationships and celebrating the love among us.

Being present speaks to the distinction between knowledge and wisdom. If you are like I was until recently, these two terms seem synonymous (Google agrees, by the way). As I have grown in my faith, however, I have time and again stumbled across compelling distinctions between the accumulation of information (knowledge) and the parsing of important and not information (wisdom). The former is about addition, the latter subtraction.

Saint Augustine said over 1,400 years ago, "We go from infancy to wisdom through intermediate stages of foolishness."

It took five decades' worth of laps around the sun for me to realize that it is much wiser—less foolish—to focus on the vital few things that make a difference rather than on the trivial many that the ubiquity of the internet and smartphones proffer. And as I wrote in the introduction, my lowercase-c universal catholic view of Christianity shows how we too often lose sight of the basics of our faith—love God, love neighbor—and instead foreground or even spar about the relatively minor distinctions among our doctrines.

Taoist author Benjamin Hoff speaks to the wayward effects of excessive knowledge in his book *The Tao of Pooh*, which allegorically employs the fictional characters from A. A. Milne's *Winnie-the-Pooh*: "After all, if it were Cleverness that counted most, Rabbit would be Number One, instead of that Bear. But that's not the way it works." Hoff describes how various Milne characters display different types of unproductive knowledge, which impede wisdom and happiness and success. In the same discussion, Hoff's Piglet says to Pooh how "clever" Rabbit is and how much "Brain" he has, to which Pooh responds, "that's why [Rabbit] never understands anything."

For Hoff, these animal-based personae are a setup for the ultimate Taoist exemplar of wisdom, Winnie the Pooh, whom the author relates to the principle of "the Uncarved Block." Hoff writes of the simplicity of an uncarved block and its "useful wisdom, the what-is-there-to-eat variety—wisdom you can get at."

I love the "uncarved block" visual, almost as much as I love Pooh. Talk about taking something big and complicated—certainly for my lifelong Westernized brain—like Taoism, and conveying it through such a clear and compelling visual. Hoff wraps up this religious doctrine and cartoon character parallelism on an upbeat note: "When you discard arrogance, complexity, and a few other things that get in the way, sooner or later, you will discover that simple, childlike, and mysterious secret known to those of the Uncarved Block: Life is Fun." I think he means *fun* in both the enjoyment and laughter way and in the "wow, I feel so alive" way. During our drive back to the compound, I think we basked in full doses of both.

As Wednesday day rolled into Wednesday night, we showered off the long day's grime (okay, I'll be honest: we were getting sort of clean, but the gradual discoloration to each of our shower towels told a different story) and put on fresh clothes and flip-flops for our evening repose. After dinner I conducted interviews with Patrick in his office and later—after our daily group debrief—with my fellow chaperones, my book research effort now fully underway.

Reflecting on this incredible day of discoveries—of no coincidences, of seeking comfort in my own skin, of trying to be present—I am amazed at how much personal and spiritual development I experienced. My mission had just passed the halfway mark, and I already felt like a changed person. God's eye was on me, and God's hands were molding my ever-pliable metaphysical clay.

After climbing into bed that night, I glanced at my email on my phone, a practice I try to avoid given the potential for something stressful to hit my brain before bedtime. The last thing I saw on this occasion, however, was a note from a former colleague who had just read *Our Way*, a flattering accomplishment, seeing as it had just been released the week before. His note was warm, complimenting the story and my writing style, and perhaps also prescient, as he concluded by suggesting I consider writing another book. So I began and ended the day under both my tattered US Air blanket and the notion that I should share my Nicaragua story.

Part 5

THURSDAY: FAILURE

*I will rather boast most gladly of my weaknesses . . .
for when I am weak, then I am strong.*

—2 Corinthians 12:9–10

20

Male Bonding

Thursday—my last full day in Pochocuape—began with a spiritual trial; Rone asked me to give the daily devotional and lead us in morning prayer. I have always been a comfortable public speaker and group facilitator, so addressing groups is no big deal. Speaking about my faith and quoting the Bible, however—and doing so before a group of adults and children, most of whose spiritual knowledge exceeded mine—was daunting. I felt like failure could be an option, and the whole failure thing and I do not go so well together. I do not like to fail.

Of course, I am not alone. The culture in which I grew up and now live does not condone failure. There is hardly any room for it. For many, grade school is about getting ready for high school, and high school—in my case, literally prep school—is *all* about preparing for college. The college transcript is about landing your first job, because *all* your other jobs depend on doing well in your first job. The cycle is established; as privileged young adults, our motivational casserole is cooked, and we approach everything with a how-do-I-succeed-or-at-least-not-fail mentality. We have become marketers, playing it safe while perfecting our personal brands on social media, *friending* people we do not know and *liking* things because it seems right to do so.

But how much do we, in our gifted circles, sacrifice from this artificially rose-lensed, avoid-the-risky-or-unpopular ethos? How much learning and growth do we miss because we avoid struggle and difficulty? Addressing the mission team on Thursday morning, I tried to relate my (our) privilege to the difficult situations around us.

We gathered in the compound's church after breakfast, and I spoke from a rectangular mahogany lectern, its lacquered surface adorned with carvings of Noah's ark, a few of the two-by-two animals, and the rainbow associated with the end of the flood. For most of my life, I found this biblical story cute and child friendly; it was only years later I realized the unprecedented cataclysm this scene signifies in Christian tradition.

It might come as no surprise that I based my remarks on Luke 12:48 (ESV), which includes, "Everyone to whom much was given, of him much will be required." I asked the group to reflect on what we had seen and done—people living in a trash dump, washing the feet of strangers, praying for multigenerational families living without electricity, playing with and hugging super-cute children, giving food to (and receiving it from!) the food-insecure, witnessing spiritual warfare at work, and on and on. Each of us gringos, regardless of age or socioeconomic status, knew deep down how much we had been given. And I think we all sensed that we were doing part of the much that would be required of us, both for the people we met and ourselves. I talked about how each of us, in our unique ways, could be leaders when we went home by modeling things like humility and compassion that we saw on display that week.

I ended my remarks with a prayer: "Dear Lord, thank you for

the opportunity to be together this morning and hopefully today to make at least a small impact on those with whom we will interact. Lord, let us appreciate the impact this experience is having on each of us—perhaps a greater impact than on the kids and communities we are here to support. Open our eyes to how the Holy Spirit works through us today, and give us the calmness in our minds and in our hearts to accept, to appreciate, and to share the spiritual growth each of us may experience. As the book of Luke says, you require much of us, and you demand much of us. Help us to summon the strength and commitment to walk in your way and to live life as your son Jesus Christ has taught us. Amen."

There was just something about that week—the people, the environment, the weather, the clothes. It was *all* about the mission, about loving God and loving neighbor. I believe these factors—together, the force of the Holy Spirit—fueled my words that morning.

Little did I know that, a year and a half later, I would be back at that same lectern preaching to over two hundred local children, trying to deliver some sort of relevant message—*in Spanish*—from the apostle Paul's first letter to Timothy. This scripture seemed apt, given that Paul was an old guy (like me) addressing a young person (like the congregation that day).

After morning prayer, sunblock application, and the proof of life, we climbed aboard our trusty cage truck and followed the Hilux out the gate and down the hill. I still dreaded that one tight turn where the shoulder drops off, my fear of heights still convincing me that the truck might list; of course it never did. Today we were heading east— away from the coast—to a remote community with which Samaritans International had connected a few years earlier. The commute wove between scattered mountain ranges and through the occasional village. We had to slow down a few times to allow small herds of gaunt cattle to cross the unpaved dirt roads, their young male shepherds guiding them with long, thin sticks they deftly tapped on the backs of the outer animals to coax the group forward. And yet another metaphor: I, too, had been shepherding and, more often, had been shepherded all week.

After crossing several large, dusty plains, we turned down a narrow, tree-lined trail to our intended destination. Another group of cattle was coming at us, paying little heed as they fanned around our small convoy and reunited in a sea of moos behind us. Up on the left, I saw a collection of tightly arranged cinder block dwellings, the residential portion of today's village. We pulled even with the homes and stopped on the right side of the road. A final cow trotted past, a middle-aged man jogging next to her having presumably retrieved a lost member of the herd—yes, more symbolism. To our right was a grove of tall trees, their dense green leaves comingling to form a large, protective canopy some twenty-five or thirty feet above the ground. Among the base of the trees were white plastic chairs occupied by a dozen or so middle-aged and elderly women clad in various bright-colored skirts, tank tops, and T-shirts.

Several groupings of children stood around the women, the younger ones staying close, the outer clusters consisting of teenagers wearing replica professional soccer jerseys. Just past the gathering was another Samaritans truck that had arrived ahead of us, carrying the musical instruments, amplifiers, and cooking equipment that were standard material for most excursions. The musical staff began performing as we walked up.

Anchoring the grove was a lone flat-roofed building, no more than twelve feet wide and twenty-some feet long. Its roof was aluminum, its walls of shipping pallets, the kind you would see in a warehouse or on the upper shelves of Home Depot. The staggered pattern of wood slats on the pallets functioned well as walls, providing airflow and privacy. Peering inside the one-room structure,

I learned that it served as community center, schoolhouse, feeding center, and church—another example of the efficient repurposing of resources at which Nicaraguans excelled.

Next to the building was the focal point of the whole scene—a large royal blue water tank, perhaps twelve feet high and six feet in diameter. Its ribbed metal form sat atop a two-foot-high concrete pad, which both elevated the vessel off the dirt and served as a nice perch where you could sit and dangle your legs; a few of the soccer shirt teens were lined up there, exhibiting the universal "we're too cool for school" behavior. Attached to the tank was a large square white sign with a blue Samaritans logo and small blue print underneath. Patrick explained that until recently this community had no local water, and the villagers had to walk several miles every day to fill large jugs to carry home. As relations grew between Patrick and the local pastor, a woman I would later interview, Samaritans purchased and installed the water tank (which a delivery truck kept full), providing a life-changing resource that was sadly considered a luxury in this region.

Reflecting on our arrival that morning, I am inspired by the practicality and ingenuity of the physical setup of the village center, proving again how necessity is the mother of invention. But I also consider the dynamics and forces that created those necessities—shortcomings in economic policy, public health, and education, to name a few. These are ways in which a community, a nation, a world has failed. Failure is a reality for too many people in too many places in the world. In my personal experience—the world in which I exist—failure is pretty rare, anathema to what life expects from what life has provided. The contrast of my privileged world and this one was again pounding on my brain and tugging at my heart.

Seeing the local men brought this societal juxtaposition into greater focus. While we had spent a lot of time with Erling, Jimmy, and other male members of the Samaritans staff, the local men—those who lived in the communities we visited—were largely withdrawn from our ministry experiences. Other than the pastor at the large church we visited on Tuesday, the few men I did see seemed to hang on the periphery of our groups, unengaged. And with so much of the focus on the children—and by extension on the women who tended them—I had not really interacted with any of the men in the communities.

In light of these dynamics, Jeff and Rone had suggested at breakfast that we male adults try to engage with our Nicaraguan counterparts on this day, that perhaps a brief connection might fuel someone's dignity or harness the power of relationship to improve, even briefly, both his life and ours. Jeff explained some of the factors impacting men's (and women's) lives in these rural settings, relating what he had learned from experts through his missionary and food ministry efforts about a connection between lack of food and brain development.

"Mental illness is a big problem," he said. "As with any part of the body, calories provide the brain with nourishment and growth, particularly in children. Food enables the brain to develop. Many of the adults—it seems more so with the men—did not receive sufficient food when they were young, contributing to their brains not developing as much as they could have. We see it pretty much every day. Sadly, you see with many of the older guys how they struggle to engage. So another benefit to providing food is that, after someone eats, although he will get hungry again later, his brain will benefit from the calories and nutrients. Food is vital."

This connection is, of course, logical, but it became more profound considering the impact it may have had on the people we saw, particularly how the men who came to our gatherings mostly hung back, seldom interacting with the group or participating in the activities. While potential stereotypes of Latin bravado may have contributed to this behavior, many of the men we saw were shy and withdrawn (maybe ashamed?) even when face-to-face with the Samaritans staffers or us gringos.

Erling, Patrick's right-hand person, told me a story from early in his time with Samaritans that underscored the sentiment of some men in his country: "We went into this community, and I saw this guy, over by himself in a corner. Everybody was singing and talking about God. But not this guy. I felt the need to go talk to him. He said he was not good enough to accept Jesus because he was a really bad person in his life. He had a lot of problems. He didn't feel worthy to be part of the group or to be welcomed by God. It really touched my heart."

Erling and others talked about how the men withdrawing impacts not only the quality of their own lives but those of others as well, especially their children, who may not see their fathers engaging in the family or in the community and could mimic such behavior later in their own lives.

In *Falling into Grace*, American-born Zen master Adyashanti talks about this generational impact: "Each of our family systems is imbued with a tremendous amount of beauty and goodness, and also carried within these systems, as we all know, is what we might call 'generational pain,' or 'generational suffering.' This is actual energy that is unconsciously passed down from one generation to the next." I believe this energy exists in different forms in every family. As a child of my parents and a parent to my children, I am humbled by—and, at times, scared about—the conscious and unconscious pain and suffering for which I am a generational conduit.

I had the chance that day in the village to interact with two men. The first, Emilio, was much older than I was. He was seated outside the gathering, hunched over on a small stool, with his forearms resting on his thighs and his fingers interlaced. My icebreaker comment was to compliment his John Deere baseball cap, its ubiquitous green and yellow logo holding up well after what looked like years of wear. I am not sure if what I did next was helpful or just strange. The week before the trip it had snowed at home, and I had a small John Deere Gator (sort of a hybrid between a tractor and a golf cart) with a snow plow on the front. While I was plowing our driveway, my wife filmed a quick video of me zooming past the back door. I played the video for Emilio and indicated with a finger point and my rough Spanish that his hat and my Gator were the same. Maybe he enjoyed seeing it, but I am not sure; his expression never changed—a blank gaze. I did not seem to connect with him. Who knows why; it could have been for any of a number of reasons. But I feel like I failed in my attempt to engage him.

Blessed with my upbringing and the life I now lead, I am mostly comfortable. This reality is why I connect so well to Luke 12:48; it grounds me in my position and responsibility. But my life has had its failures, ranging from the personal to the professional. As a boy, I valued sports more than any other activity. I was obsessed with playing sports and competing, whether for a school team, at summer camp, or by myself in the driveway. My favorite memory of this latter type was as a preteen, pretending I was pitching for the Philadelphia Phillies—in game 7 of the World Series, of course. I used a tennis ball and threw it at the gridded pattern of our wooden garage door, the center square mimicking a strike zone.

While I never "lost" game 7, I did experience the first major setback of my athletic career around that time: being cut from the seventh-grade basketball team. It threw me for a real loop. I did go on to play four varsity sports in high school (including basketball) but experienced more losing seasons than winning ones and missed my last high school season due to a knee injury. So I was around failure more than success in the activity I cherished most as a child. I recognize that this level of failure pales compared to actual life-altering childhood failure like major health problems, economic struggles, or the loss of a loved one. But my experiences were my experiences; for me, they were tough setbacks, stabs into the core of who I thought I was.

The other man I met that day in the village was Vincente. Vincente was younger than Emilio, maybe around my age, and was standing next to one of the trees in the grove, his hands shoved into the pockets of his gray khakis. What drew me to him was his smile—a rare expression among the men I had seen. He was smiling because our group was performing a song called *"El Gato y el Ratón,"* a catchy tune about a cat and a mouse. The staffers set up a game where one person plays the cat and another the mouse. The rest of the group forms a circle around the two players. The objective is for the cat to catch the mouse. As the music starts, the group allows the mouse (played on this day by one of the local boys) to escape the circle, which then pulls together, locking arms and even legs to prevent the cat (played by my roommate, Charles) from getting out. The cat moves from gap to gap trying to breach the circle.

Charles was awesome. He tried to push between people, dive between legs, even jump over arms. He did it all with unbridled enthusiasm, knowing how much everyone was loving his making a complete fool out of himself. When Charles finally did escape, the mouse easily reentered the circle, forcing Charles to repeat the breaching process all over, only this time with his hat turned backward, indicating he now *really* meant business. When the song mercifully (for Charles) ended, he collapsed in the dirt, huffing and puffing inside his now sweat-stained grayish blue SWH T-shirt.

At that moment, I saw Vincente quietly chuckling and swaying back and forth at the absurd behavior of Charles, a similarly aged man. Vincente's smile—and his eyes—radiated a joy that belied the hardness of his wrinkled, leathery face. As the din of the postsong cheering subsided, I went up to him and, motioning to Charles, said, "¿*Es loco, no?*" (He's crazy, isn't he?). Vincente answered, "¡*Pues sí, muy!*" (Well yes, very!). We introduced ourselves and exchanged a few basic phrases about the people and the weather.

Unlike Emilio earlier, my interaction with Vincente felt positive, like we united across the many gulfs that divided us. In this case, the human spirit—expressed through humor—created a memorable connection, hopefully for both of us. But I need to point out that Emilio and Vincente were each alone, not interacting with other local men—and more tellingly—not with any of the children.

While there was a smattering of men present at most of our gatherings, none seemed to be parenting the kids, leaving me to wonder about a failure of family dynamics: I know what a problem single-parent households are in the US, where the majority of the time it is the dad who is not present. As the product of and father in a two-parent environment, I worry about the impact this lack of male role modeling and influence has on both boys and girls—both in the US and in places like Nicaragua.

21

Short-Term Missions

The brevity of my interactions with Emilio and Vincente stirred an important debate about short-term mission trips: Do they work? Are they effective? Or do they create more issues and contribute to more inequality? Are they more failure than success?

David Livermore's *Serving with Eyes Wide Open* wades into these waters, asserting a mixed viewpoint of such efforts:

> While the life-changing impact of these trips on the locals is used as a way to motivate people to support the trips, little research has explored whether short-term trips really help. . . . Most of the reports about the positive impact on local communities come from North American participants and sponsoring organizations, not from those who received the participants.

Livermore's questioning is supported by discussions I have heard on missions questioning whether the financial investments (and ecological footprint) required to send groups from developed countries (e.g., air travel, local guides and protection, food preparation, 500 milliliter water bottles) are as sound an investment as channeling those funds directly to the local communities. Many mission trips (although none on which I have gone) focus on construction, perhaps of a schoolhouse, church, or water system. The above logic suggests that hiring locals might be better than using kids from the States; the locals may actually have applicable skills, and their employment would help the economy.

These arguments are often rebutted in part by a theme I have promoted in this book, that the North Americans doing the mission work are beneficiaries as well. One expert contends "we are building kids, not buildings," echoing the idea that taking the time to travel, live in austere conditions, and interact with different people expands not just American kids' comfort zones but their propensity for helping others as well. But Livermore cites research that questions the lasting impact short-term missions have on our kids. At a minimum, he advises to "resist the temptation to overstate our level of impact" and to "step back and serve with eyes wide open."

These economic and attitudinal challenges may indicate a level of failure (at least failure of meeting expectations), particularly for the more skeptical observer. While I appreciate these perspectives and agree that everything should be done with eyes wide open, I—along with my fellow chaperones and leaders—see indisputable value for everyone involved. This value is largely why I wrote the book you are now holding.

Jeff chimed in accordingly: "I challenged Jimmy on a trip last year, asking him sincerely, 'What impact are we really having?' I was debating if it's mostly impact for us [Americans]. I think it's a genuine question.

"Jimmy did a good job of pointing out things throughout the trip. He pulled me aside at one point and said, 'You see that right there [referencing an American teen playing with a local child]? That's maybe changing that kid's life.' He said, 'It's the relationships you're building. You have no idea the long-term impact it's gonna have.'"

Jeff continued: "Servants With a Heart is a different mission trip than one that would build a school or a water system. I've been on those types of trips, and they're really hard physically. But you're not building relationships as much. The way our trips are structured, it's all relationship focused. It's that one kid, whether it's the one Jimmy pointed out last year or any kid that one of our folks interacts with, that's the whole purpose of our trip. It forces relationships, which matter even if only for a few minutes."

Jimmy has seen many missions come and go during his two decades of ministry. He highlighted the effect on the visiting kids by the end of the week—the time our trip was approaching: "On the last night before a team leaves, I like to focus on the kids that are shy and maybe haven't said much all week. When it comes their turn to say their highlight of the week, they find their voice. They find that it didn't take the latest iPhone or PlayStation. They say something like, 'It was that little four-year-old boy. I grabbed his hand and carried him on my shoulders for a while. That was awesome.'"

Jackie from Samaritans concurs: "At first, many kids are shy and maybe spend the days not feeling much. But by the end, they really feel they came here for a purpose. I mean, wow. You can see it from the first day to the last day. They are friendlier, they can feel open to hug people and deal with people. It's really amazing how people, even kids, can change here, can feel empathy for people."

As you should gather by now, the students were not the only visitors benefiting from this work. Jimmy talked of returning chaperones telling him how interacting with the Nicaraguans made them better people. "When they come back on a return trip, they say how they appreciate just a hug or a handshake so much more. They say how they just want to go out and hug someone. It's love."

Patrick, the leader of Samaritans International for the prior eight years, addressed the concern that short-term mission trips are failures—or at least underachievements—for the locals. As he spoke, his passion increased, making his rural North Carolina accent more and more pronounced: "I've been told this from a lot of books and people during my time that short-term missions don't work. Well, this is what I can tell you. The people here look at it as a great honor for Americans to come into their community. They come in and play with their kids, bring food for their families. We have found that the food opens doors all across the country. People listen more once they are fed. We've had whole communities where we walked in and no one knew Jesus, but now the community is Christian; they are now walking with Jesus. That's an amazing thing. Now their faith makes them stronger and better able to handle their tough situation. And the Americans being here helped make that happen."

Rone drew on parallels from his Special Forces experience, when counterinsurgency and nation-building efforts entailed similar but secular approaches: "It's the same sort of approach we used to integrate with other cultures. You go into their community, you try to hang out with them, to be culturally aware and sensitive to what's important to them." He was also clear not to overplay religion in our efforts: "The worst thing you can do is start thumping the Bible. If you look at what Jesus did, he always started with the relationship first, the same thing we're doing here, right? Work on relationship first, and address the hunger, then maybe you can have *that* conversation." I learned over the course of these discussions that the food was often the better door opener, while the Word—and the spiritual nourishment it could deliver—brought a different but also vital form of comfort.

Rone's comment about "Bible thumping" leads me to a related disagreement within Christianity, one of those topics around which there is much ecumenical debate: whether believers are saved (and therefore able to go to Heaven) by declaring our faith in Jesus or if we must back up that faith with good works—the things we do in our lives. Generally speaking, many Protestant and evangelical doctrines subscribe to the former, Catholic teaching to the latter.

While I am always up for a good theological discussion about scriptural interpretation, I believe if you are committed to living a Christian life, you should have strong faith *and* aspire to act as Jesus taught (good works), including employing the concepts I talk about in this book. What we do and how we treat other people should not change, regardless of which side of the how-to-punch-your-ticket-to-Heaven divide we occupy.

The issues our work in Nicaragua raised—who benefits from missions, how money is best spent, what the value of a relationship is—are nuanced and complicated, evoking both the science and the art of outreach and human interaction. So maybe it's understandable how short-term mission trips may not live up to their pre- and post-trip hype. If planning is inadequate or your motives are wrong or myriad other forces go awry, things—and maybe people—could end up worse for the effort; failure is an option. I was fortunate not to experience a mission like this in Pochocuape. As I write today, with my sample size of three, I come down on the side that short-term missions—done right—are meaningful and profound experiences for all involved.

After Charles's *gato* display of enthusiasm and self-deprecation, a few more songs were sung and games were played. During this time, I caught a glimpse of Jeff seated on the edge of the water tank platform, his lower legs dangling and the heels of his sneakers idly tapping the concrete wall. I detected the slightest grin on his face. He appeared to be taking in the entirety of the scene, perhaps reflecting on the melding of cultures, the universality of music and play—or perhaps, greater yet, about all that Samaritans International and Servants With a Heart had created or perhaps even more about the beauty and wonder of humanity. Maybe all of these things were running through his mind. Or not.

I asked him later, and he said he was simply smiling at what a fool Charles had made of himself. It made him feel good to see his dear friend rolling around in the dirt for the amusement of others. Okay, maybe I had failed by overdramatizing his reflective pose. But smirking at Charles is still fun!

After the music ended, we formed an assembly line from the cooking area to the grove, where the people were gathered to hand out the bowls of warm food. We served the smallest children first, and I approached a tiny boy no more than three years old. He was standing between the knees of (presumably) his mother, who was seated in one of the plastic chairs, her straight-faced expression not giving anything away. Mom appeared to be about twenty years old and was wearing what looked like a Little League baseball T-shirt from the States. The toddler had on a gray collared shirt, blue and orange shorts, and the tiniest pair of Crocs I had ever seen. As I bent down to his level and extended the food, he reached up with both arms, and our hands touched briefly. When I said, "*Jesús te ama,*" the corners of his mouth turned up ever so slightly, the blessing appearing to register. Mom's demeanor went from neutral to warm, a thin smile and head nod indicating approval.

Before we left, the team handed out boxes of uncooked food to the local families, and I interviewed the village pastor (again via a translator), who was also the schoolteacher (for all grades) and the de facto mayor. She related a somber state of affairs in the village: "There are real challenges. Most of the parents here, they don't work. And most of the kids that I have here at the school, they don't have food. So many times they ask me like, 'Teacher, when are the gringos with the rice coming because we have no food in our houses?'" I had heard this term, *gringos with the rice*, before from Jeff and the other J-term veterans. Erling was quick to point out that it was not a term of disrespect but merely descriptive. It became part of our chaperone lexicon for the balance of the trip and over subsequent phone calls and email exchanges.

The pastor painted a picture of suffering—in this case, a lack of employment prospects and insufficient food. While much of the blame for such hardship stems from broader economic and societal ills, I feel like I saw glimpses of relevant guilt on the faces of some of the Nicaraguan men—namely, Emilio—even if little blame for their situations lay directly at their feet.

But suffering and hardship also spawn a heightened awareness of and appreciation for things that may otherwise be taken for granted. The village pastor embodied this counterintuitive by-product in her follow-up comments: "So these people all feel very happy when I tell them you are coming. The packages of food will help sustain them a little bit." When we finished our conversation, she gave me a surprisingly strong two-armed hug, its force squeezing instant tears out of my eyes. Her concluding words and warm embrace were an authentic, human way to conclude my time in that community.

22

Life through Lenses

We returned to *Embajada del Cielo* for a quick late lunch. Our afternoon would be spent moving furniture in the compound's classrooms, which were unfortunately vacant of students given that it was still their Christmas break. The school is a key part of Samaritans International's support of and investment in the local community; they provide free education for close to two hundred local children, ranging from preschool through high school. Patrick had acquired new desk and chair units for the elementary grades' classrooms. Our job was to remove the current furniture, load it onto a truck, and place the new pieces in the classrooms—good use of our physical labor. When I say the units were "new," I use the term in a relative sense; they were certainly not fresh from the factory. They were, however, in better condition than what the school currently used; the upgrade would surely be noticed when the students and teachers returned the following week.

This exercise presented another perspective-broadening experience, as it is unlikely any of our J-termers had attended schools where new furniture was, in fact, not new. I heard a US Army general speak years ago who used the expression "better is better" to describe how anything you do, if it improves the situation, is worthy of your time. Improving the situation for those students, coupled with the bonding among our group that common physical labor produces, qualified as "better."

Rone gathered us together as the classroom work concluded and informed us that for our last night we would be going to Pizza Hut for dinner. *Really? How ugly American is that? If we are venturing out, shouldn't it be to some authentic local haunt?* Then Rone explained that it had become a tradition to take out the Samaritans staff and their families for a thank-you dinner at the end of the trip, and the staff preferred Pizza Hut for this splurge meal, a place reserved for special occasions, including, I believe, the wedding reception of one of the staffers. In understanding that my privilege caused me to look down on a restaurant that was a treat for others, I had to ask myself, *Well, Mr. Smartypants, who's the ugly American now?* I felt about two feet tall.

Everyone showered and rested, then loaded into the vehicles and headed down the hill to dinner. Several of the staff, some of whom I did not recognize—a sign of how much went into supporting us— were already seated at tables arranged in a U shape around a reserved section of the restaurant. We agreed to sit among the Samaritans staff and their families. I sat next to the wife of one of the drivers, while many of our kids beelined to seats next to those guides with whom they had become close. The dinner was a lot of fun, our group consuming pizzas and pitchers of Coke and Sprite about as fast as the wait staff could replenish them. A few people offered remarks to the group, the most memorable being Patrick acknowledging his employees' young children who were there, causing a few of them to lean shyly behind an adjacent mom or dad. The evening felt intimate, an appropriate way to wrap up a week centered on relationships.

But my afternoon knee-jerk reaction to our restaurant choice still stung. My presumptive ignorance was another example of failure. I allowed the life I had lived and the settings I had known to fuel my reaction, even after those intense days of immersion in a life so different from mine. I saw how my worldview was dominated by my own experiences. I saw the narrowness of the lens I used. Lenses—either the eyeglasses I wear or the paradigm I employed to judge the restaurant—help us see but also dictate our vision.

Life coach and motivational speaker Rob Scott talks about lenses' obvious yet profound effect:

> A lens is built to alter what we see; we all know that is its main function. But the other thing is it's built to be invisible. People don't always get that. It's literally built to be looked through. All our thinking and our beliefs are lenses, built to alter what we see and to do so invisibly. Political beliefs, religious beliefs, beliefs about myself, and so on—they're all lenses.

Scott goes on to say how lenses are necessary and normal, but "our attachment to our lens is what leads to disagreement and even to war. It's what leads to relationships completely dissolving."

This negative outcome of lenses reminds me of a friend who once told me she had become less religious (she is Christian) and more spiritual, citing that she had found it increasingly difficult to connect with the Bible because it was written by men, and the woman's point of view is lacking. It took me a while, but I eventually saw her point. While a few books are titled after their plots' female protagonists, it is unlikely that any of the Bible was written by women.

As I mentioned earlier, women for most of history had few rights and few opportunities for education and advancement, including acquiring the ability to read and write—let alone to have their writings taken seriously. So my friend's point illustrates that much of history, including the Bible—the book at the center of the most popular religion in the world—was recorded through a male lens. It is understandable how this one-sided interpretation could leave women wondering about the past and their true place in it. And while I now understand how this concept of lenses may have weakened my friend's relationship with Christianity, I hope she has not let the unchangeable context of biblical authorship overly drive her away from the multitude of beautiful teachings the book offers.

My objectionable reaction to the Pizza Hut announcement provided—as many moments of failure do—a learning opportunity. I believe in the expression "the truly educated never graduate"; part of life's continuing education is learning to admit our mistakes. *New York Times* columnist Tim Herrera calls learning opportunities part of a "failure résumé." "Falling on our face gives us the rare opportunity to find and address the things that went wrong (or, even more broadly, the traits or habits that led us to fail), and it's an opportunity we should welcome. . . . Analyzing one's failures can lead to the type of introspection that helps us grow." This growth process is what I love about Catholic confession—reflecting on ways I have failed to act in accordance with my faith, admitting those mistakes out loud, and attempting to atone for my wrongdoings.

I have been fired from jobs twice in my career—once as a bartender during a college summer and once as a company president in my family's business. The first time was the result of my accidentally placing in my tip jar two dollars left on the bar to pay for two beers; a spotter saw what I had done and reported the incident to the owner. Even though I had been a good employee for two seasons and had simply made a mistake in the weeds of a happy hour drink special, the rules were the rules, and I was unceremoniously fired around two a.m. at the end of my shift. Was that a learning opportunity? The two dollars certainly did not make or break my summer earnings. Maybe I learned that sometimes an honest mistake is still a mistake, and repercussions can occur. Or maybe, as David Brooks says, "Failure is sometimes just failure (and not your path to becoming the next Steve Jobs)."

My other firing—perhaps not the perfect word here—happened in my early thirties. I had been running a large part of our family business, and while some good things were happening, the business was not keeping pace with the market and struggled to make budget—two table stakes for being a president. My brothers had the unenviable task of removing me from the role, concluding rightly that I had on blinders; I was not performing, and my lens was preventing me from seeing clearly. It took a lot of courage for them to do what they did. We planned and announced a transition, and I moved to a new role that better leveraged where I was in my career path.

That failure rattled me, and it took me the better part of a decade to recover professionally. As I said earlier, I had not experienced much adversity in life, certainly nothing as visible or with as many people's livelihoods at stake. There is a concept in secondary school education to the effect of "little kids, little mistakes; big kids, big mistakes," implying that it is desirable for people to experience adversity when they are young, since the consequences are typically not as dire as when they are older, but the seeds of resilience are still sown. I did not have many early setbacks. My career path and track record to that point lacked moments of hardship and suffering; there had been no adult versions of being cut from the seventh-grade basketball team to harden my resolve for the bigger stage of failed performance ahead.

I learned key things about myself and my leadership style, most notably to remain open to divergent information and opinions and to be flexible when conditions or behaviors are not what they were planned to be. So while I did fail in the role, I ultimately did not fail to learn from the failure. I grew from that experience as much as I have grown from any phase of my career. C. S. Lewis wrote in *The Problem of Pain* how God uses our trials to get our attention: "We can ignore even pleasure. But pain insists upon being attended to. God whispers to us in our pleasures, speaks in our conscience, but shouts in our pains: It is [a] megaphone to rouse a deaf world." So it seems that the biggest failure about failing would be not to learn from the experience.

Circling back to "little kids, little mistakes," how much do we parents let our children fail? To set your daughter or son up for adversity runs counter to the core parenting tenets of safety and protection. What I see more than failure scenarios for my children— and for the J-termers in Nicaragua, for that matter—is pressure. Young people today experience forces that my generation did not have to endure. Developed-world expectations about grades and college, about extracurricular activities and youth sports, coupled with the novel pressures of social media and personal brand perfection take an insidious but dangerous toll on a young person's psyche and self-esteem.

How many people ever share publicly that they are having a bad day or post an unflattering picture of themselves? No, the opposite is true: People glorify the events in their—and their children's—lives, and they pay for and use various filters to enhance images so they are always the best version of themselves to friends and followers. All of this enhanced reality builds up imperceptible steam inside a young person's figurative pot, which may rupture in unpredictable places at unforeseen times. Again, these developed-world pressures differ from those in other regions, including other parts of the United States, but they are real and cannot be ignored or belittled.

So failure is not an isolated event but three parts unfolding: First is how much people are set up for or allowed to fail, especially children and especially in places of resource and privilege. Second is the act of failure itself, falling flat on our faces and hoping the consequences are manageable. Finally and perhaps most importantly is the learning from failure, how we pick ourselves up, dust ourselves off, reflect on what the heck just happened, and move forward.

Our closing dinner at The Hut created a nice bookend to the washing of feet that helped launch our trip; we started and ended with recognitions of dignity and expressions of gratitude for our hosts. We returned to the compound and gathered in our small groups, having the children start to summarize and coalesce their experiences from the week, the final step of the "Telling Your Story" exercise Rone introduced Sunday night. This would be my last time with the group; I was leaving a few hours ahead of them the next morning for my trip to Philadelphia.

Recall that the exercise was in part designed to help us answer the "so how was your mission trip" question. The emerging themes I heard Thursday night from the students gave me a sense for what their answers would be: "a life-changing trip," "deep connections even without speaking the language," "sharing hugs, smiles, and kindness," "no matter where you live, you can always help others," and perhaps my favorite, "seeing pure joy through the love of Jesus Christ."

Considering these likely takeaways, I reflect on the outgrowth and learnings that our trip, so far out of any of our comfort zones, might produce, and more broadly how adversity—and failure—have contributed to my career, my family, and my faith journey. How have I been set up for adversity in my life, and how much (or how little) have I allowed my kids to fail? How have I handled the failures I have experienced, one of which required almost a decade of recovery? And most importantly, how have I grown as a person from failure and what have I learned about myself and about life?

On these last questions, I think most strongly about the nebulous but vital concept of grace, which to me is part of both humanity and divinity. Grace is most needed and thankfully most present when circumstances are not ideal, when failure is a possibility. On a human level, I see grace as the ability to comport yourself and convey respect to others, regardless of your circumstances or how you were treated. My mom exhibited tremendous grace, whether it was making others feel appreciated, opening her home to friends and strangers alike, or putting on a happy face even when she was not feeling well or had been wronged.

I spent much of my life (and still do at times) prioritizing justice and fairness—noble pursuits, for sure. But as I crest midlife, I find that my desire for righteousness and accurate scorekeeping can be counter to my relationships, at odds with how I should treat others— especially since I do not live in a glass house. Being right can be wrong if the outcome unduly damages the relationship. My mom understood this. As my temporal odometer clicks along, I hope to better honor her example.

Grace is also divine, a direct gift from God. This powerful, gratuitous gift provides us with the inexplicable ability to traverse life's obstacles and leap life's pitfalls, regardless of how big the climb or deep the drop. I like the notion that grace is receiving what we don't deserve while mercy is not receiving what we do.

A boy I know from home is battling sarcoma, a life-threatening form of cancer that caused him to have his left leg amputated. His family has used a social media site to post updates of his journey (a very good use of social media), including their reliance on God and faith to handle their trials: "In our current situation," they wrote, "so many people are saying, 'How can you handle all this? I could never do what you are doing.' [My son's] friends are thinking, *There is no way I could accept all this if I was him.* Grace says you don't need to handle it, because this situation was not given to you. You don't know how we are handling this because you were not given the Grace to accept this exact situation. *But we were!* And that is how we are handling this, by the Grace of God."

She concluded her entry by quoting from Paul's second letter to the Corinthians: "'My Grace is sufficient for you, and my power is made perfect in weakness.'"

Adyashanti's *Falling into Grace* deals (obviously) with this same topic. "The aspect of spiritual life that is the most profound is the element of grace. Grace is something that comes to us when we . . . are willing to entertain the possibility that we may not know what we think we know . . . [when] somehow the difficult situations in our lives have a way of opening our hearts and minds the most." He calls this "the suspension of any conclusion," which relates back to the serenity of knowing what we can and cannot control.

I saw many instances on my mission trip of people enduring difficult situations, and I believe the grace of God enabled them to persevere. Witnessing struggle and failure broadened my mind and opened my heart to the challenges and realities of the world beyond my daily horizons. Fortunately, these scenes were accompanied by moments of gratitude as well, including several during my trip home the next day.

Part 6

FRIDAY: GRATITUDE

Every time I touch food, whenever I see a flower,
when I breathe fresh air, I always feel grateful.

—THICH NHAT HANH,
Living Buddha, Living Christ

23

Godwinks

I had trouble fathoming my day of departure had arrived, perceptions of space and time muffled beneath the week's tropical layer of faith and mission. I awoke with relative ease to my predawn alarm, the day's logistics front-of-mind. I considered the bizarre fact that that evening I would be in the bleachers of my son's high school basketball game—two thousand miles and an indigestible amount of contrast away.

Recalling how frugally I had packed for the trip on Sunday morning, I was about to set a new personal standard for traveling light. Part of Jeff's pretrip suggestions was to consider leaving in Nicaragua articles of clothing, medicines, and other effects for Samaritans to donate. I selected a few items of clothing with this charity in mind, setting aside most of the SWH shirts (Jeff recommended donating all but one), along with a pair of shorts and a few medicines, and commenced loading my Rollaboard. I placed my flip-flops in first . . . and then paused. *Do I need these?* I love wearing flip-flops, but the pair I had brought were one of I-am-actually-not-sure-how-many pairs I owned. Maybe I should leave them for someone who actually has zero pairs of flip-flops—or maybe of any footwear? Out they came.

The flip-flops started a trend of reconsideration. First one pair of shorts, then two, then all of them. (I was wearing my lone pair of pants, which I had worn on the trip down.) Next was my trusty khaki hat. Then a few newer pairs of socks. Then my unworn rain jacket. And finally, the trail shoes that had walked me all over Nicaragua that week (I wore sneakers home). The low-top boots were dusty but had plenty of miles left. I was struck by the adage of "walking a mile in someone else's shoes" as I snapped a photo of remembrance of them.

I now had a decision to make. I was leaving far more stuff than I was taking; my backpack was only half full, and my larger bag was nearly empty. Without thinking much about it, I loaded everything coming with me into the backpack and everything staying into the suitcase, which would now stay behind as well; Jeff and Patrick had been adamant that they could repurpose anything we left. As I zipped closed my longtime traveling companion for the last time and left it behind in the room, I had the feeling of Tom Hanks's character in *Cast Away* when he realizes that he and *his* longtime traveling companion, Wilson the volleyball, would be forever separated. A tad overdramatic, but hey, I was swimming in emotion.

Reflecting on this moment of antimaterialism, I am reminded of a line from the preacher character in Steinbeck's *Grapes of Wrath*: "I never seen nobody that's busy as a prairie dog collectin' stuff that wasn't disappointed." While I still did—and do—have a habit of "collectin' stuff," deciding to leave so much in Pochocuape lit an ember of internal warmth and lightened my load, literally and figuratively. It's interesting how easy it was in a developing part of the world to convince myself I didn't need something but how hard it is to ask the same question about something in my Amazon cart.

Jimmy drove me to the airport—a pleasant symmetry for my time at the compound since he had also brought me from the airport on Sunday, a drive that felt like months ago. Ten minutes into the trip, his cell phone rang. Patrick was calling as Jeff and Charles awoke to see my full suitcase sitting in the middle of our room and assumed I had forgotten it. Jimmy relayed my intentions and hung up the phone.

This quick series of events softened the already warm rapport between Jimmy and me—one final cracking of the shell. Our early morning conversation wound through topics of faith and family. Most poignantly, Jimmy said, "I would like to add that working with missionaries has changed my life. I want to continue helping others through ministries like this." What struck me was Jimmy was the one helping others, but he seemed like the one benefiting. He seemed like the one who got something meaningful out of the logistics and mission duties he performed. He seemed grateful.

Gratitude is the final theme from my six days. Being grateful, thankful, appreciative, obliged (I wish the term "much obliged" was still in vogue)—simple concepts and likely the easiest to grasp of any in this book. Someone does something nice for you, and you say thanks. Something happens that causes you to reflect on the good things in your life, and you feel fortunate. A "nice guy" finishes first, and it warms your heart. Any exchange of this sort—literal or symbolic, stated or implied—unites people. Gratitude is an elixir for our conjoined souls, a bonding agent for humanity. Being grateful is as much at the core of relationships and love as anything I know.

Motivational speaker Rob Scott bases much of his coaching gratitude, in part contrasting our human focus on desire, which creates a state of lack and want, with our focus on gratitude, which creates a state of abundance. One of Scott's cooler phrases is "What fires together wires together," meaning that the neural pathways in the human brain will respond to the thoughts and emotions they transmit. If you emphasize negative things on a regular basis, your brain will wire together around the negative, whereas focusing on positive things—centered on gratitude—will have the opposite effect. Scott says that "as we think certain thoughts, neurons start to bundle and tighten up. We all have both sides of this coin. If we've been ruminating on negatives, we've been basically growing a big, old thick highway of suffering. If we can start to break that process and instead go into gratitude, that muscle can grow really well. Then gratitude comes up much more naturally in our daily lives. It becomes much easier to experience it."

Scott's "Hacking Happy" self-guided program on gratitude focuses on developing habits around positive thoughts, baby steps toward increasing the gratitude in your life. Having not done much in the way of meditation or mindfulness to that point of my life, I found the program useful and inspiring.

At the core of any gratitude practice is choice. I have to *choose* to focus on being grateful and on the good. Far more of the world is set up to show us the bad and scary, the dangerous and sad. I do not mean to be Pollyannaish or diminish the struggles around us (my week in Nicaragua in particular) but to suggest being more open to the positive and more grateful for healthy ways to balance the trials and tribulations life throws our way. Scott says, "Why can't we move our attention to what is amazing? It can be as simple as *the sun came up*. Or *nobody's punching me right now*. Or, *wow, I have clothes on*. Whatever." On that morning drive to the airport, I was grateful for Jimmy, simply for being next to him and sharing one final slice of faith pie.

After passing through security, I settled in for the two hours remaining before my departure. Three moments stuck out. The first happened while I sat in an airport café having breakfast. While the food was decent and my Spanish conversation with the waiter flowed freely, what I recall most is the music playing from the recessed speakers in the ceiling: British and American classic rock, played loud, the way I like it—The Rolling Stones, The Who, The Doors. Timeless hit after timeless hit, the music initiated my transition back to my world. Author Squire Rushnell coined a term for such happenings: *Godwinks*. Continuing with my earlier theme that there are no coincidences in life, I look back on that Friday morning breakfast soundtrack as a small Godwink—a little nod from above that it was time to go home.

The second notable preflight moment involved social media. I first joined Facebook in the late 2000s to accept an invitation for a high school reunion. Soon after, I joined LinkedIn and Twitter, given that my responsibilities at work included marketing. At the time of the mission, my social media presence was plain vanilla—postings of my wife on her birthday, pictures of a tasty meal I had prepared, and so on; I never put myself out there as far as divulging core elements of my personality or beliefs, particularly to my growing cadre of Facebook "friends." I decided, however, while sitting in the airport to publish a series of pictures I had taken of people on the trip, titling it "Faces of Nicaragua," the location of the post being the Managua airport. While my captions were not in-your-face Jesus material, this post was my first time illuminating my faith in such an explicit way. I was nervous clicking the "post" button but felt compelled to start incorporating faith into my social media presence.

The final key moment from the airport involved an unpleasant topic I discussed early in the book: toilet paper. Having spent the week at *Embajada del Cielo*, where we could not flush paper products and had to collect and deposit them in an outside trash can, I was oddly joyful to discover that the airport toilets were paper-friendly.

As I later waited in line to board the plane, I texted Jeff and Charles—my roommates and fellow joke crackers—that the airport flush "was everything I ever dreamed it would be."

———

Settling into my seat for the flight to Miami, I said a prayer to ask God for safety for our plane and, more importantly, protection for my family should something happen. As I have discussed, the power of prayer took on an entire new meaning for me on this trip. While I had prayed my whole life, my prayers were of the textbook sort—asking for certain outcomes or reciting memorized stanzas—on my knees in church (low lighting, soft organ music), at the dinner table before a formal meal (Norman Rockwell–esque), or in bed at night (hands clasped, eyelids pressed).

More recently I have begun praying anywhere and everywhere—in the car, on a walk, at the kitchen sink, right now while I am typing. Prayer has become a dialogue with God, and like any conversation with someone close, it no longer requires a certain body position or reverential location. God provides advice and direction, perspective and conscience, and companionship and joy. I need all those things all the time, and I am grateful for the permanent earpiece into my mind and into my heart.

Praying with others can be impactful as well, as I experienced during the many examples I described in this book. I returned to Pochocuape about a year and a half after my initial visit, and during this second trip, the power of prayer took on a whole new meaning. I was asked to preach to a church of about two hundred local children and many of their parents. Prior to my time to speak—which I did in a mix of Spanish and English with the bubbly translator Jackie by my side—a Samaritans staffer led the congregation in a heartfelt, tear-evoking hymn. A local teenage girl then performed a beautiful barefooted dance wearing a flowing skirt and decorative shawl, both of which billowed in circles as her arms and legs followed the rise and fall of the accompanying music. The congregation was rapt . . . and I felt doomed. My body tightened. I started shifting my weight foot to foot. The few folks I knew gave me sympathetic, "tough act to follow" looks. Then one of my fellow missionaries spontaneously put his arm around me, pulled me close, and prayed to God to send the Holy Spirit to give me the strength to deliver my sermon.

And guess what? My muscles relaxed. My mind cleared. A warm calm came over me. While the words I then shared perhaps did not match the song or dance that preceded me, I know my friend's prayer helped me meet the moment.

A greater display of the power of prayer during this second trip involved a church we visited deep in the Nicaraguan rainforest— during the rainy season. It poured hard every day, to the point where even waterproof rain gear and moisture-wicking apparel became soaked. As we entered the tiny church, I again became aware of my privilege, noticing how none of the locals had rain-resistant clothing, only umbrellas of varying sizes and quality that thwarted only some of the deluge. I realized I could deal with wet hair and damp socks.

During the portion of the gathering when we prayed over the attendees, Patrick, Samaritans International's leader, offered petitions for two different women, both of whom were older and complained of physical ailments. With the first woman, Patrick placed his hand on her back where she said it hurt; her face contorted. Upon touching her back, Patrick recoiled and grabbed his own lower back. The extreme of his back arching and ceiling gazing and guttural yelp took me by surprise. But he composed himself and told me (in English) and the woman (in Spanish) that he sensed she might have had a kidney infection. She nodded her head. With no viable healthcare options (so I was told), the afflicted often relied on people of faith for comfort. Patrick told me such infections were common due to the varying water quality in the more remote regions of the country.

He then held the woman's hand with one of his hands and placed his other hand on her back, leaned his forehead into hers, and began to pray. His words oscillated between Spanish and English, and his tone and emotion increased steadily during the two or three minutes that he prayed. Eventually one of the other Samaritans staffers moved behind the woman and stood with his arms extended. As Patrick's words reached their crescendo, the woman started to shake, and her knees buckled. The staffer calmly absorbed her weight and guided her down to the floor. She lay there motionless for several minutes with her eyes closed and tears streaming down her cheeks. But she wore the faintest smile. I struggled to process it all. The woman then came to and with the help of a few locals, sat up and moved to a nearby seat, a placid expression now on her face.

Patrick then moved to the second *abuela*, who complained of abdominal pain. He told me it was not proper for him to touch the woman's midsection, so he had a female staffer do so, and he held that woman's hand. Once the three-person chain was connected, he recoiled again. Maybe her bladder, maybe a UTI—again, likely caused by polluted water. Patrick's praying this time, while still bouncing between Spanish and English, also included indecipherable sounds and phrases. I realized he might have been employing the charismatic practice of speaking in tongues, just as Jesus's early apostles did in the book of Acts.

Witnessing this scene, while standing in a small, hot church in the dense jungle, with rain pounding down on the shallow aluminum roof, I was more than a little freaked out. After a few minutes (I guess it was a few minutes?), Patrick motioned for me to stand behind the woman. I crouched down, arms extended. Sure enough, her legs bent, and she melted into my arms. In this case, however, she did not go down to the ground but instead lay against me for five or ten seconds and then stiffened, righted herself, and stood straight. She nodded to Patrick and the Samaritans staffer, gave me a slight smile, and shuffled off into a group of close-quartered women.

So what was ailing either of these women? Did Patrick help them feel better? Could prayer have been that powerful? Tough questions, for sure. But I know what I saw, and I sensed relief in each of those believers after our brief but intense interactions. I believe what happened that afternoon was divine.

Rounding out my thoughts on prayer, my brothers and I recently took a long weekend "guys' trip" to bond with our dad, who was several years a widower. While we are all Christian, religion plays a different role in each of our lives. We worship at different churches, and each of us is in a different place on his faith journey. We spent time one afternoon in fellowship, reading a piece of scripture and reflecting as a fivesome on its meaning. What stuck with me from the conversation was our responses to a question that evolved from the reading: What is a one-word reason you go to church? I loved our answers then, and I love them now: peace, hope, education, nourishment, happiness (mine was nourishment). Five pretty good motives—Godwinks, even—to go to church, to connect with the Lord, to pray.

24

Faith Walk

As the flight toward the States continued, I found myself reflecting on my faith journey. This was likely the first time I had considered my life experiences worthy of a religious theme. For the most part, I had not thought holistically about this path; events and learnings had been mostly isolated occurrences, disjointed moments of Christianity slotted into their defined and appropriate places in my time on earth.

Since that time, I have invested a lot of time and energy reflecting on my faith journey. Today I am as grateful for this walk as I am for anything in my life. My faith has evolved to be the inspiration and the road map for who I am, for what I value, and for how I act. For me, faith and gratitude are two sides of a most precious coin.

Raised Episcopalian, I went to church (mostly) every week during the school year, with admittedly pleasurable summer respites. I attended Sunday school and learned the Ten Commandments and that Jesus died on a cross. I learned about Noah's ark and remember drawing crayon pictures of the big boat, the animal couples, and the rainbow overhead—mystical symbols of a God and a religion to which I was exposed on Sunday mornings for an hour or so in a mostly reverent, if perfunctory, fashion. I remember the feeling of elation on the car ride home, peeling off my jacket and yanking down my tie, quietly noting—pun intended—*thank God that's over with until next week.*

Other than an extended family wedding every few years and a smattering of middle school bar mitzvahs, I only ever worshiped at our church. And going to a nonsectarian private school, I had little exposure to faiths outside my own. My recollection of Passover was that it was some sort of special meal Jewish people had around when we celebrated Easter. On this point—and I'm embarrassed to admit it even today—my mom once reminded me about a time we were driving a friend of mine home in elementary school and I asked him, "Hey, are you Jewish or regular?"

Even with my limited exposure to religion outside of the Episcopalian Church, I developed a prejudice about Catholics. Mostly I recall not liking the concept of "Catholic guilt," how it seemed their doctrine approached human behavior not from points of positivity and hope but from points of admonishment and the idea of catching you doing something wrong. I had Catholic friends throughout my schooling but never engaged any in substantive conversations about faith. My biases sat latent for years.

Everything changed a year after college when I met Kelly, a lifelong Catholic who as a child spent a portion of every Saturday night saying confession at home with her uncle Frank, a Roman Catholic priest. She earned undergraduate and graduate degrees from Villanova, a Catholic university, working in the Religious Studies and Education Departments while going to school. She and I fell quickly in love, and the religious difference was not high on our radar.

During our engagement, we attended Pre-Cana, the Catholic Church's marriage preparation program. While the content was helpful, I recall being relieved when the sessions were cut short by a snowstorm. We also met with the rector of my Episcopal church, whose Jesus-esque long hair and thick beard made him seem right out of central casting as a spiritual guide. When I posed our Protestant/Catholic dilemma, he told us that with many of the couples he counseled, he was hopeful to find one evident faith, but with us, it was reassuring that we had two, so we should focus on our commonalities to navigate through our (what appeared to me as big) differences.

Uncle Frank, aka, Father Eigo, would officiate our 1997 marriage at Villanova's church, generously offering to have my Episcopal minister co-officiate and deliver the homily. A sticking point would be deciding whether to include Communion, the point in a Christian service where bread (the Eucharist) and wine are blessed and shared with the congregation. While all Christians believe in Communion, only confirmed Catholics are supposed to receive the bread and wine at a Catholic Mass.

Uncle Frank was fairly progressive and had told me months before the wedding that if I felt "predisposed as a Christian" to take Communion in a Catholic church, then I should. This advice was contrary to Catholic teaching but gave me, I concluded, the air cover I needed to receive the Eucharist. Kelly and I nonetheless opted to take Communion privately with Uncle Frank the day before the ceremony rather than create unwanted tension by having most of Kelly's (Catholic) guests receive and most of my (Protestant) guests remain seated.

My minister's homily centered on the concept of a child tending to a butterfly with an injured wing, his point being that husband and wife need to learn when to help each other fly and when to leave the other alone to sort things out, still good advice twenty-five years later.

While Kelly was pregnant with our first child, we discussed how we would raise him or her (no, we did not want to find out the gender in advance with any of our kids). Kelly was understandably clear that any child of hers would be raised Catholic. While this was not my preference, I knew how much deeper her faith was than mine. Uncle Frank baptized all three of our children before he passed away. While we were not weekly church attendees for our first two decades of marriage, we mostly attended Catholic masses. I recall feeling disconnected, sensing a rote cadence to the services and the congregation going through the motions. I was reluctant to participate in many of the group recitations, nor would I make the sign of the cross—the tracing with your hand of an imaginary cross from your forehead to your heart and shoulder to shoulder. And I never attended Mass alone.

The next major—and perhaps greatest—mile marker along my faith journey occurred in June of 2015. My mom had been battling a series of afflictions in her later years, including gastrointestinal distress; she was one of the first people we knew to develop celiac disease, now so common. Cardiopulmonary issues exacerbated her condition, and she and my dad spent long spells traveling the East Coast, seeing various experts and clinics in search of treatments and therapies, to little avail. The years of illness led to months in and out of hospitals and eventually to days of ICU and, ultimately, the decision to send her to their home in Florida with hospice care. Many of the family flew down to be with her. The ascent of my flight was terribly rough (recall that I used to be a nervous flyer), but I concluded (even at that less advanced point in my faith journey) that God would not possibly take me then, knowing where I was headed.

I arrived at my parents' home on a Saturday afternoon. Mom was in the large bedroom at the end of the house, lying in a hospital bed that had been delivered earlier in the day. After a blur of hugs with family and close friends—all hunkered down for the vigil—I dropped to my knees at Mom's bedside and grabbed her hand. Some words of affection poured out of me, but I don't remember what they were. Mom was not able to talk, but she acknowledged my presence and what I was saying through changes in her breath and light movements of her head and hand.

As Saturday night became Sunday morning, we drifted in and out of her room, mumbling beings not knowing what to say or how to act, only sure we didn't want to stray far. At one point I tried to sleep for an hour or so on the daybed in her room, but needless to say, no one was getting any real rest as Sunday unfolded.

Mom's hospice nurse, Emi, was amazing. She administered pain medication when needed, and she calmly instructed us about what was happening to Mom's body at various points, including what signs she was looking for—like specific color changes in her feet and alternations in her breathing pattern—that would show Mom's ultimate time was near. Emi said that Mom was unlikely to make it through another night. Hospice care providers are incredible. I consider them angels in nurses' clothing given how they care for the patient *and* for the family at life's most difficult moment.

While some of the family in the next room mindlessly picked at Sunday night supper, I sat with Mom. Emi then said the words I had been dreading: "Bill, it's time." I went out to convey the news. I'll never forget how quickly and uniformly everyone shot up from their seats. We all gathered around Mom. We called our family members up north and laid the phones by Mom's head. Each of us took turns saying our final goodbyes. Then, just as Emi had said she would, Mom took her last few breaths . . . and she was at peace. I was holding her arm. It was incredibly sad. But it was incredibly beautiful as well, my mother surrounded by family, a warm sunset filling the large sliding glass door by her bed, and the unmistakable presence of God when her suffering ended. My sorrow was of course deep and raw, but the awesomeness of God's presence—the Holy Spirit—was unmistakable; I felt a warm connectedness to everyone—family, friends, and care providers.

Mom's passing changed my life, not only for the obvious and inevitable fact that I lost a parent, but for the events that ensued, how God started to guide me from that moment. Within two months I decided to transition out of most of my duties at our family business and focus on researching and writing *Our Way*, the biography on my father. Within six months I was attending fellowship meetings with him and starting to think about forming a men's group with some of my contemporaries. Within a year a group of us did just that, convening early Friday mornings to discuss the Bible and how it applied to our lives. All but one of us has known each other since we were young kids; the "new guy" has been in our lives for *only* twenty-five years. I eventually started a second small group and regularly participate in a third.

Catholic priest and Christian scholar Richard Rohr writes in *The Universal Christ* how losing a loved one can change you:

> In the days, weeks, and years after a great grief, loss, or death of someone close to you, you often enter [a] unitive mind. . . . The magnitude of the tragedy puts everything else in perspective, and a smile from a checkout girl seems like a healing balm to your saddened soul. You have no time for picking fights, even regarding the stuff that used to bother you. . . . You are reconfigured forever. Often this is the first birth of compassion, patience, and even love, as the heart is softened and tenderized through sadness,

depression, and grief. These are privileged portals into depth and truth.

I still have work to do with things like anger and being comfortable in my own skin, but my mom's passing did seem to soften my heart and perhaps reconfigured me. It may seem incongruous to associate gratitude with my mom dying, but I am grateful. I was grateful then that her battle was over and that she reunited with my sister, Karen. And I have been grateful every day since for the grace and life skills she imbued in me and for the spiritual path that her passing illuminated, including putting me in Pochocuape and compelling me to pen this book.

I changed planes in Miami, where the process of going through customs was easier with no checked luggage. It did feel strange traveling after a weeklong trip with just a backpack. The first person with whom I interacted was an airport employee at the entrance to customs. I asked her how to get to the domestic terminal for my connecting flight but perceived that English was her second language and my words were maybe not registering. I repeated my query in Spanish, and she kindly told me which set of roped aisles I should enter. Walking away, I smirked at how my time south of the border facilitated my initial exchange on US soil.

Once in the domestic terminal, the first store I passed was an airport spa, one of those pop-up spaces with a few face-forward massage chairs near the hallway. What caught my eye, though, was a row of cushioned chairs along the back wall, three or four of which were occupied by other travelers. Their bare feet were placed in basins of water, and spa attendants were seated low, giving them pedicures.

I was now back in the States, the pinnacle of the developed world, and the first group activity I witness was, yes, washing of feet. The juxtaposition stopped me in my tracks. My week started with us washing the feet of those who would be taking care of us—doing what Jesus would do—and was now ending with the exact opposite dynamic in a south Florida airport. Sometimes God's messages are hard to notice, but this one was easy—a big ole Godwink right in front of me. I still smile today thinking of God's irony and sense of humor.

On the flight to Philadelphia, I continued pondering my faith journey and how grateful I was for God's presence in my life. A year or so earlier, in one of my first fellowship meetings with my lifelong friends, I remember sharing how Kelly and I had recently been through a tough stretch in our marriage. After working things out, we sort of restated our vows, albeit informally, sitting alone on our sofa one morning. This reaffirmation of "'til death do us part" reinforced Kelly as the central relationship in my life.

In the fellowship meeting, I asked where Jesus fits if Kelly is my primary relationship. One of my friends said to picture Jesus giving Kelly and me a big hug. The visual was perfect, just what I needed to reconcile faith and marriage at the time. Today, however, I am comfortable saying that my relationship with Jesus is the most important bond in my life. While this technically bumps Kelly to second place, my relationship with her is stronger, an indication that the closer I have become to God, the stronger my connection to my wife (and to all those important to me) has grown.

Christian author W. Paul Young has a cool related analogy in *Lies We Believe About God*: "Jesus introduces us to something completely different: a moving, dynamic, living relationship in which God is not first but central. This is not a flowchart but, rather, a mobile, where everything is moving and changing as our choices and participation are woven inside the activity of the Holy Spirit. . . . If God is at the center of our lives, then so is love and relationship, since God is profoundly both. God doesn't want to be first on your list but, rather, central to everything."

My relationships, not as a flowchart but as a mobile, with God the central weight and focus? Sign me up!

The same friend who gave me the hug analogy likes to call our weekly sessions "spiritual weightlifting," another apt metaphor—in this case, for how the work we do in small group makes us spiritually stronger as people of faith. Our relationships with each other and with others grow stronger. There are certainly many people who have in-depth relationships not centered on God. But I know that the deepest bonds I have—the people with whom I am most vulnerable—involve shared faith.

It is not hyperbole to say that, in the years since my mom passed away, my entire view of Christianity and religion has changed. While I still retain the cinematic G-rated visuals of Noah's ark and the animals and the rainbow, their beauty and cuteness are tempered by the R-rated realization that the flood wiped out the entirety of humanity except for eight people. The rainbow afterward might have been God's reminder not to hit that massive restart button again. In recent years I have learned that Passover, which had been for me an unknown Jewish meal, commemorates a night when the angel of death *passed over* the homes of the chosen people—who had been instructed to paint a stripe of animal blood on their front doors—while killing the firstborn of all other households. Similarly, right after Jesus was born, he and his parents fled their hometown under the cover of night because the ruling king, threatened by the possibility of a powerful religious figure in his kingdom, decreed that all males under the age of two should be murdered. This updated, adult version of Christianity has gotten my attention.

The cross—the most important symbol in Christianity—has ceased being some benign, esoteric image from my youth; it has become a grueling, graphic device of torture, employed when the authorities in ancient times wished to exact the most painful and prolonged death by torture. During the time of Jesus's crucifixion, Roman authorities would often scourge the criminal, whipping his torso with a rope of sharp objects to open gaping wounds and commence the dying process. After driving large spikes through the person's wrists and feet to hold him on the cross once it was erected, the executioners would often break his legs, rendering the victim unable to support his body weight; the position of his arms would then constrict his chest, causing him to suffocate relatively quickly. With Jesus, however, no bones were broken, and He lasted an unimaginable three hours suspended to the cross before dying. Needless to say, my Sunday school teachers in the 1970s treaded lightly around these details and their significance to our faith.

With this better understanding of what a crucifixion entailed, I now see the cross as the ultimate symbol of the unimaginable agony Jesus endured for our sake. The cross I wear around my neck is a constant, grateful reminder of His sacrifice, invisible to others beneath my shirt but in constant contact with my heart—where it belongs.

My recent faith journey is about a lot more than new realizations of life thousands of years ago. What used to be an hour each week focused on God (or at least sitting in church) has evolved to a 24/7 commitment to try to live as Jesus taught, focused on loving God and being in close relationship with those around me. I have

Psalm 116:9 pasted to the bottom of my computer screen (next to Luke 12:48, as I explained earlier): "I shall walk before the Lord in the land of the living," to keep me on this path. Very little of Jesus's ministry took place in houses of worship. Most of his meaningful acts were in poor communities, on open roadways, and in nature. Similarly, I view the Christian life I live *outside of church* to be more important than the standing, kneeling, and signing I do for an hour every Sunday morning at Villanova Chapel.

25

Closer Connections

A recent big stride in my faith walk was the decision to convert to Roman Catholicism, the same denomination about which I had held such bias for much of my life. I deliberated over a long period of time, mostly to myself, in what people of faith call a process of discernment. Then a series of events occurred in quick succession—God's plan for me unfolding.

One early fall weekend a few years ago, Kelly and I were at Mass, and I noticed two of the Eucharistic ministers, members of the parish community who assist the clergy during the service. The couple were neighbors of my dad's, in their eighties, and Catholic. I noticed how seamlessly they coordinated their duties and was struck by the bond between them, its strength having been forged in houses of worship like the one we were in. I thought, *How great is that?*

My observation seemed isolated until I had dinner a week later with a work colleague, also a lifelong Catholic. I relayed the story about the couple, how cool it would be to have that with Kelly, but how I did not know if I should convert. He responded with a simple question: Did I love my wife? *Well, duh. Sure I did.* He went on to share how meaningful it was to worship with his wife, particularly in their empty-nest years. On the drive home, I wondered about committing more fully to a church community and started to believe that the Catholic Church—with Kelly as my partner and ally—might be the place. Another stepping-stone on my path was illuminated.

In sharing these two couples' stories with my fellowship group, one of them cautioned me to commit to a church not primarily because of what was best for Kelly and me, but because of what was best for *me* first, where I would feel closest to God. I view such a connection as a push and pull: simultaneously pushing to be a better version of myself, to be—as I said earlier—who Jesus would be if He were me, coupled with being pulled, or grounded, by a foundation of beliefs and principles like the ones in this book. This combination centers me, makes me feel more engaged in life, and gives me confidence that I am making a difference for those around me.

As my journey continued and my spiritual weightlifting made me "stronger"—in this case more willing to share my discernment process with others—the next key event unfolded: a parents' cocktail party for our daughter's grade. The gathering took place as a new round of unthinkable sexual abuse acts and cover-ups in the Catholic Church emerged. While speaking with the mom of one of my daughter's friends—who works at a Catholic elementary school—she offered a lens to view the crisis that helped immeasurably, suggesting that I consider viewing the purity of the faith as something distinct from the people who had interpreted and exercised that faith over time. She discussed how, throughout the stories of the Bible and the two thousand years since the time of Jesus, men and women have regularly interpreted God's messages for their own earthly convenience, straying from the example Jesus gave us and trying to justify their actions—or worse, conceal their or others' actions—in the name of faith.

Later in the evening, I spoke with one of the other dads, who had been raised Protestant and converted to Roman Catholicism about a decade earlier. He told me his story and how after learning more about the faith, it just *felt right* to become Catholic. I sat on the couch across from him, listening to his words while processing what the mom had said earlier. The gears in my head and in my heart were turning.

I shared these stories and my deliberations with Kelly. She listened and was supportive, appropriately not providing an opinion other than I should do what I believed was right. I then finally summoned the courage to email the pastor of St. Thomas of Villanova, our parish where I was a one-foot-in-and-one-foot-out attendee. In my email, I introduced myself and gave a brief outline of my story, asking if we could meet. Father Joe responded warmly and accepted my request.

The week of our email exchange was the same week that a Pennsylvania grand jury issued its scathing report of ongoing and pervasive sexual abuse by Catholic priests across the state. These unthinkable acts—and the equally reprehensible cover-up tactics by certain Church leaders—were and are unfathomable and inexcusable. Because you know that I now believe there are no coincidences in life, I think God willed me to contact Father Joe that week. If—as the woman at the parent gathering had said—I could ever see "the purity of the faith as something distinct from the people who have interpreted and exercised that faith," now was the time. Some of the men who had become priests had violated this purity in the most twisted ways imaginable. If I was ever going to parse the noble teachings from the flawed practices, now was the time. I sensed that, perhaps, this was God's way of telling me now was my time, when the gigantic and seemingly infallible institution of the Catholic Church was on its heels and ripe for needed transformation. Perhaps God wanted to use my talents and gifts to make some miniscule impact.

When I arrived at Father Joe's office, I first noticed he wore a navy blue cardigan sweater—and so did I. I then noticed a guitar perched in the corner. I had started playing the guitar a few years earlier. Hmm. Same sweater. Both play guitar.

Father Joe and I had a wonderful conversation about my faith journey and my discernment process. He is from the Bronx and combined a bit of the New York gruffness that I have come to appreciate with a kindness and ability to connect—also qualities of many New Yorkers—that made me instantly comfortable. He offered that if I decided to convert, he would work one-on-one with me in the process.

After about an hour, we shook hands, and I left his office. Upon exiting the parish center, I walked down a path next to the chapel, and I wept. I did not sense the tears coming, but they came, not big sobs but watery eyes, lumpy throat, and instant runny nose. I thought: *This is it.* Just like Dena explained at breakfast that one morning in Nicaragua, this was the Holy Spirit at work. My decision was made.

Over the next few months, Father Joe and I met weekly to discuss Christianity and how Roman Catholicism dovetailed with and varied from my childhood teachings and life experiences. I learned a tremendous amount. Our discussions were far ranging and enjoyable; perhaps my not being a "cradle Catholic" facilitated my independent views and naïveté to bring up just about any topic. Father Joe allowed me to schedule my confirmation while my oldest son was home from college so the whole family could be present.

I am a thorough decision-maker, often rightly accused of being overly analytical in my data collection and deliberations. In the case of whether to convert to Catholicism, my discernment led to a concise but important list of pros and cons. Topping the latter category was the above pattern of abuse, with my decision to separate the perpetrators and accomplices from the faith's purity, allowing me to proceed. Also on the cons list were the fact that priests cannot marry—a restriction that I consider a contributing factor to the abuse—and that women cannot hold the same clerical positions as men. While I understand the historical context of both of these stances—including that a priest must marry himself to God and Church and, as I have discussed, that the roles of men and women varied greatly throughout history—I continue to wonder whether and hope that one or both of these practices will change.

I would also prefer that baptized Protestants be permitted to receive communion at Catholic Mass, provided—as Uncle Frank put it—they feel predisposed to do so. The reason the Catholic Church does not support non-Catholics taking communion centers on transubstantiation, a mouthful term signifying the Catholic belief that the bread and wine actually *become* the body and blood of Jesus Christ. Most Protestant denominations that celebrate communion believe that the bread and wine represent Christ but do not actually become Christ. I understand the importance of the distinction but would love to see a way for other devout Christians to join us at the Lord's table.

With these concerns, you might ask—as even Kelly did—why I decided to convert. Most important is that I began experiencing—and still feel—a closeness to God through the Catholic faith and during Catholic worship that I had not felt before. And I feel more connected with my wife and kids (all Catholic), my favorite moment of every week being listening to the homily with my arm around Kelly.

The Catholic Mass, which had previously seemed rote and even mindless, became an active time of participation and reflection, where the words and hymns and rituals resonated in my mind, heart, and soul. I developed a profound appreciation knowing that I could be in virtually any Catholic church, anywhere in the world, and the congregation would be reflecting on the same scripture and performing the same sacred rites. I started occasionally attending early morning Mass alone, an experience I find uniquely nourishing. I do not recall ever leaving Mass and not feeling like I had grown as a person or somehow worked through something internally.

One of the priests at my church, before offering communion—the very climax of the service—holds the bread and wine in the air and bellows, "See what you believe! And become what you see!" This reminds me that Jesus died for my sins and that I should live my life as He wants. One of my favorite Mass prayers is the expression of faith called the Nicene Creed—or its close cousin, the Apostles' Creed—which provides a concise and compelling tribute to the Holy Trinity: Father, Son, and Holy Spirit (many Christian denominations recite these prayers, by the way). At one point, the Apostles' Creed wording says about Jesus, "Born of the Virgin Mary, suffered under Pontius Pilate." Richard Rohr calls the punctuation between these two phrases *the Great Comma*, noting how that one small grammatical symbol encapsulates over thirty years, the entirety of Jesus's life and ministry.

Also on the pros list is that I was—and am—drawn to the passion of the Catholic faithful. One expression of this devotion is the size of Catholic congregations, filling churches even in summertime, when—in my experience—many Protestant churches are decidedly empty. As I mentioned above, perhaps I can play a small role amid this size and commitment in helping spread God's word and a greater appreciation for relationships and love. Rounding out my reasons to convert was the fact that Catholicism's roots trace back to Jesus's apostles and the founding of Christianity—the original Church. Even with the warranted reformation movements launched by

Martin Luther and others in the 1500s protesting what they deemed to be insufficient focus on scripture and flagrant abuse of Church powers, I appreciate the line I see from today's Roman Catholic Church back to Peter and the earliest practitioners of Christianity.

A few months after being confirmed, I sustained an inguinal hernia, a somewhat common abdominal injury often resulting from lifting something heavy or overexerting yourself physically—two stubborn hobbies of mine. Fortunately, the repair surgery is minor, as far as procedures involving general anesthesia go, and mine went off without a hitch. But the benign outcome belied the mystical gravity of the experience.

When I was brought into the waiting area, a friendly pre-op nurse introduced herself as Karen. I thought: *Neat. My sister's name was Karen, and she had had a number of procedures in this hospital.* As I sat on the bed in my pre-op bay, the anesthesia nurse came in and introduced herself. Karen. *Two for two.* The third and final nurse I saw before surgery—the operating room nurse—also introduced herself—yup, Karen. Three nurses, all named Karen, in the very hospital where my sister had been many times in her life. My nerves were calmed knowing that although Karen had been gone almost twelve years, she was looking over me.

Most people who have been put under for surgery recall the odd, in-and-out sensory experience of waking up as the anesthesia wears off. My recovery room résumé had included four knee surgeries and a set of wisdom teeth, so I was familiar with the feeling. After the hernia repair, however, the first thing I recalled was different: My eyes were still closed, but I sensed a light in front of me, emitting warmth. With my mind's eye I saw an image standing in front of the light source, diffusing the brightness. The blurry image had long hair, a bearded smile, warm eyes, and wore a robe . . . Jesus, just like I pictured He would be. Even in my semiconscious state, I felt secure.

For the next few minutes or seconds—I don't know—the backlit image moved from the center of my mental field of vision to my left and then faded into the distance, causing my neck to rotate that direction. As the image disappeared, I opened my eyes for the first time and was staring right at Kelly, her face exactly where Jesus's image had dissolved. He had handed me off.

Thank you, Lord.

The final Godwink of my spiritual surgery was after gazing at Kelly and sensing the relief we shared. I noticed two new nurses standing at the foot of my bed. One asked how I was feeling, but I answered with a question of my own: "Your name isn't Karen, is it?" She said, "No." Before I could process her response, she motioned to her colleague and said, "But hers is."

Thank you, sis.

26

Live Nice

After completing an uneventful but reflective flight to Philadelphia, I shouldered my backpack and headed up the Jetway. If bad things can come in threes, maybe good things do as well. My two good things from the Miami airport—the language-barrier bridge with the customs agent and the dichotomy of the pedicures in the spa—were about to get their third.

In the middle of the walkway between terminals B and C, a long, wide, store-lined thoroughfare with welcoming rocking chairs next to charging stations, was a gospel choir in flowing white regalia belting out a hymn, their full-throated tones and sweat-soaked foreheads signaling the passion and energy with which they were celebrating God. *Have they been here before? Have I just not noticed? Or were they put here today for me?* I didn't know the answers but in hindsight believe the Holy Spirit nudged me to walk past them to show that the presence of God and passion of faith I had experienced in Central America also exist in my hometown, that the call to honor the love of God and neighbor is visible and audible everywhere, so long as I am willing to look and listen.

That night I had the enjoyable but surreal experience of watching my oldest son play in one of his final high school basketball games, against his team's archrivals no less. The contrast of experiences—and awareness of the blessings I enjoyed being able to travel so far to make the game—weighed on me. I was physically in a large gymnasium but emotionally in Pochocuape, the sights, sounds, feelings, and even tastes and smells of the mission still present. I admit to feeling shock seeing the two teams in their professional-looking uniforms, on a perfectly shellacked wooden floor, beneath halogen lighting in a temperature-controlled environment. But knowing my firstborn was about to compete brought me into the moment.

Our student section for home games is always full of boisterous teenagers cheering on their classmates on the court. Each game, the students select an attire theme, such as bathrobes or Western attire or, regrettably, jorts. On this night, however, they had selected a holiday theme, given the early January date. Dubbed "Silent Night," the crowd chooses not to cheer—to remain silent—until the home team scores their tenth point, then they go crazy. When the game began, I truthfully didn't notice their hush as I focused on my son. But when my son scored the tenth point on a put-back basket, the crowd erupted. Unaware of the Silent Night custom, proud papa here thought the deafening roar was *entirely* for my son. And of course I teared up. Anyway, our team won the game, and the seniors on the team and their families went out for a late dinner to celebrate. The evening was a final exclamation point of gratitude for a day—and a week—that gave me so much about which to be thankful.

I am even more thankful now. As I complete this book, our society is shrouded in the most devastating pandemic in a century, the worst economic crisis since the Great Depression, the strongest calls for racial equity and social justice in fifty years, and grave natural catastrophes. In one sense, a story about handing out some food in Central America seems insignificant. But given today's world-altering, world-focusing events, perhaps my sojourn in Pochocuape is as fitting as any experience could be.

I now see what I learned in Nicaragua in much clearer focus. Displaying good character, including integrity, humility, and hard work, is foundational for how we should act. Recognizing the inherent dignity in every human being and celebrating that dignity may be the most generous thing we can do for our neighbors, both in our communities and around the world. We should all determine what difference-making talents and gifts we have, then make those differences, guided by the serenity of knowing what we can and cannot control and influence. We see failure all around us; I know I have failed during the pandemic in how I have reacted to the world around me and how I have treated others. Learning from those failures makes me a better person. And finally, in a time like this one, with its unprecedented challenges, heartaches, and obstacles, I am more grateful than ever for the people in my life and the faith that guides me.

One final piece to this puzzle of how to live is to *live nice*, a phrase that a friend of mine's daughter coined after incessant queries from her dad about being nice to everyone, always: "One day, after the thousandth time my dad asked me this, I said, 'Dad! How about I just *live nice* from now on?'" She sells T-shirts with the phrase and donates the proceeds to various charities in her area. I believe living nice entails both the Golden Rule (treat others as you would like to be treated) and its updated sibling, the Platinum Rule (treat others as *they* would like to be treated).

Living nice speaks to the importance of civil discourse, of how even though we may disagree, we should commit to understanding before being understood, to being open-minded and thoughtful, and to being civil in our interactions. According to Jennifer Knust, professor of religious studies at Duke, "Any opportunity to try to find some kind of common understanding and some kind of meeting ground where we can share what we love, even when it's different, seems to me a necessary human goal in a divided world." And when we inevitably trip up in our interactions, the apostle Paul advises that we "be kind to one another, compassionate, forgiving one another as God has forgiven you in Christ." In short, live nice!

———

Discerning why each of us is here—our purpose—is both basic and profound; reflecting on our lives is a regular exercise, but assigning a fitting and compelling meaning to who we are requires curiosity and introspection. How should we interact? How might we better steward resources for the future of God's creation? How could we discover our purpose? For me, it took losing my mom, changing my career, committing more to my faith—and traveling to Nicaragua—to open my eyes to a different path and a reordering of what mattered.

In *Love Does*, Bob Goff, after reflecting on the band of unlikely individuals from the Bible whom God called to acts of great faith (like Moses, Peter, and Paul), challenges his readers about purpose: "So the next time God asks you to do something that is completely inexplicable, something you're sure is a prank because it requires a decision or courage that's way over your pay grade, say yes." Writing this story seemed above my intellectual and spiritual pay grade, but the Holy Spirit—and my fellow missionary Dena's goose bumps at breakfast—compelled me to do it.

I believe this biographical journey has been part of my purpose. Relating my own and my fellow missionaries' experiences is part of how God is using me to make the world a better place. Perhaps this book is a tiny step on the path toward what Pope Francis recently described as "a new society . . . based on service to others . . . rather than the selfish scramble by each for as much wealth as possible; a society in which being together as human beings is ultimately more important."

Everything I have shared has been in service to relationships and love. Relationships are the conduits that transport and nurture love. And love is a higher power—actually, the *highest* power. I believe in this power, down to my core.

Love is about service. I learned so much in Nicaragua about how to connect with others. By stripping away what I thought mattered and learning to love with a servant's heart, I experienced community and connection in remarkable and unprecedented ways. What a privilege that was.

Love is a privilege beyond all privilege. I believe love compelled me to spend six days in Pochocuape and to write about it. Maybe love is part of what compelled you to read this book. I am grateful you have. My hope is you might engage a little more in the world around you. Maybe you will invest a little more in the relationships that matter. Maybe this investment can lead to sharing more of the love that exists among us. Maybe that is our purpose.

In Nicaragua, I saw God's hand at work—and *was* God's hand at work. I was a minister and was ministered to. Spending the week two thousand miles from home taught me how to treat and honor others—not just in a foreign land but in my daily life and in my own communities. Reflecting on everything that happened, I feel nourished. I feel at peace. I am happy. And so I honor María's attitude at the trash dump, encapsulating the power of God's grace and living a life fueled by unvarnished faith:

Yo estoy contento.

Acknowledgments

I want to first offer gratitude to my brother Jeff and his wife Suzanne for founding Servants With a Heart and encouraging me to travel to Nicaragua. You two live by the adage that Christianity is a contact sport as much as anyone I know. I'm proud to contribute all of my net proceeds from the sale of this book to Servants With a Heart.

I want to thank the staff of Samaritans International, led by Patrick Brown, and my fellow chaperones, Dena Brown, Rone Reed, and Charles Roebuck. Your tireless and God-driven commitment to help the less fortunate opened my eyes and my heart to what true servant leadership looks like.

To the brave and faith-filled high schoolers who did the lion's share of our mission work, your authenticity and compassion showed me what God means when God says we need to live more childlike. To the countless (and largely nameless) Nicaraguans with whom I interacted, your resilience, your warmth, and your faith—yes, your unvarnished faith—have forever changed how I perceive others and how I gauge what truly matters.

I want to thank the many friends, colleagues, and classmates who walk with me on the faith journey, whether in fellowship, gospel reflection, or graduate studies. Among the many clergy, spiritual guides, and professors who mentored me in the production of this work, I am particularly indebted to Uncle Frank, Father Joe Genito, Rev. Frank Allen, and Margaret Mell for your teachings and your modeling of how to walk purposefully. And to the many authors and scholars—present and past—whose works I have cited, your wisdom and writings helped develop my faith lens and form the words I have offered here.

To both of my independent editors, Kimberly Ford and Robert Noland, your expertise and often contrasting viewpoints compelled me to think more deeply about what I believe and therefore what I wanted to say in these pages. To Gunnar Rogers and Abby Ellis, thanks for your promotional and digital insights and professionalism. And to the team at Greenleaf, particularly Nathan True, Pam Nordberg, Leah Pierre, Chase Quarterman, Morgan Robinson, Danny Sandoval, and Chelsea Richards, thank you for transforming sixty-some-thousand words of text into a beautiful piece of art, making this story and its messages more accessible to more people.

Last, I am eternally grateful for my family. To Mom (always looking down on me) and Dad, my siblings—Hal, Mike, Jeff, and Karen (standing next to Mom)—and my entire extended family, your support and your grace helped me develop the curiosity and confidence to embark on journeys like this. To Kelly and our children, Will, Colby, and Russell, I would not be a writer without your unyielding encouragement and counsel. My published works are as much yours as they are mine. You are my Godsends and my Godwinks, every minute of every day.

Reader's Guide

OPENING

1. Why do you think Bill led with the opening story? What do you make of Maria's answer: "I am happy"?

2. As Bill introduced the book—what religion is, the centrality of love and relationships, an overview of the story to come—what resonated with you? What missed the mark?

3. Think of a memory or experience when you felt particularly loved and connected. Why was that? Are there conditions (people, places, experiences) that lend themselves more to support and connection? How might those dynamics be replicated elsewhere?

4. Bill introduces universal ideals of faith, including the centrality of love and relationships, applying our abilities and resources to help others, and honoring God and loving our neighbors. How do you see these in play (or not) in your community? What contributes to their presence or absence?

PART 1: CHARACTER

1. Bill shares poignant examples of how strong character is made up of integrity, humility, and hard work. Do you agree? Is there anything you would add? How have you witnessed these attributes in others?

2. Can you think of a recent time when you had the opportunity to show strong character, whether you succeeded or failed? What did you learn?

3. What do you think is meant by "integrity carries the burden of courage"? In what ways did Jimmy demonstrate this?

4. How do you relate pride and humility? Do you see one or the other more prominently in yourself? In your community? Should there be space for both?

5. What does it take to be a hardworking person? How do you distinguish worthy endeavors from busyness?

PART 2: DIGNITY

1. Why do you think dignity matters to Bill? What role does it play in his story?

2. What does dignity look like to you? How do you find dignity and fulfillment in your work or studies?

3. What are some concrete ways in which you can recognize and honor the dignity in others? How do you reconcile honoring another's dignity with differences in identity or ideology?

4. What do you think of altruistic egoism? How have you seen it at play in your life?

5. Bill says that "so many Americans choose to be unhappy and complain, not in spite of our materialism but in light of it." In what ways does abundance reduce our compassion or foster a negative mentality? How might we combat this?

6. "Perhaps dignity expressed by action is more authentic than dignity expressed by words." How did Bill and his companions express dignity by action? How can you? How can nonverbal communication express sentiments in ways words cannot?

PART 3: TALENTS

1. Bill writes that the central duty of a person of faith is to use one's talents to help others. What are your unique talents and gifts, and how do you employ them to make the world a better place? Where or when do you fall short in offering your talents and gifts?

2. What are some seemingly ordinary talents that can make a big impact (like the chaperones applying temporary tattoos to give children a moment of joy)?

3. Bill writes, "Happiness can come in all forms . . . perhaps the less material, the better." Do you agree? Think of an experience in your life where you felt overwhelmingly happy. Why was that? How do you see material things helping or hindering happiness?

4. Discuss what Bill means by Christianity being a contact sport. How can you expand on this analogy? What forms could "contact" take? How has the pandemic changed things?

5. Bill writes that this trip was a two-way street, that the members of the mission learned just as much, if not more, from the locals, and that the chaperones learned from the kids. In what ways did you see this in action as you read the story? How might this be true in your own life?

6. "What do you give the person who has everything? You give them time." How could you do better at giving your loved ones time? How could you do this for strangers? What else could you gift to someone who materially has everything they need?

PART 4: SERENITY

1. Bill describes his journey to become comfortable in his own skin. How comfortable are you in your skin? Do you find yourself "putting on perfect" as well? Where (or with whom) would you like to improve?

2. Do you believe there are no coincidences? Why or why not? How might this differ from "everything happens for a reason"?

3. How would you describe faith? In what ways does it help you make peace with uncertainty? Have you had conversations with others whose faith perspective is different than yours—or absent? What did you learn?

4. What can you learn from Bill's story about the toothpicks? Are there any times in your life you wish you had been more present? What can you do when you find yourself hyperfocused on the past or future to bring yourself back into the moment?

5. What is the difference between knowledge and wisdom? What is an area of your life in which this distinction could be useful?

PART 5: FAILURE

1. Part 5 opens with the following verse: "Most gladly, therefore, I will rather boast about my weaknesses . . . for when I am weak, then I am strong" (2 Corinthians 12:7–10). How can you see your weaknesses as strengths? Or rather, how does acknowledging your weaknesses give you strength?

2. In chapter 20, Bill debates the effectiveness of short-term missions: would the resources spent on outside aid be better invested directly into the local community? What do you think?

3. When was a time you failed? Can you reframe this failure as an opportunity to learn and grow?

4. When was a time you avoided doing something because you were afraid to fail? How might you recognize and combat this anxiety next time?

5. What privileges do you have that you don't readily admit? How does this impact your life? Any learning opportunities for you?

PART 6: GRATITUDE

1. Bill writes that being grateful is at the core of relationships and love. What do you think he means by this?

2. How have you seen gratitude in action in the book? How about in your own life?

3. Reflect on the book's discussion of how gratitude and desire relate to feelings of abundance and lack. How do these relationships play out in your communities?

4. The book talks about gratitude as a practice, that "what fires together wires together." Have you experienced people or situations where thankfulness has had a compounding effect?

5. What are you grateful for today? Think about big, wonderful things as well as what might seem like small, trivial things. How might gratitude for smaller things impact your routine and your outlook?

6. What does it mean to "live nice"? What resonated with you from Bill's description? Would you add anything? Can it be hard to live nice in certain situations or around certain people?

CLOSING

1. Beyond character, dignity, talents, serenity, failure, and gratitude, are there other tenets you believe are vital to living a life of faith and meaning? Why?

2. What can you do today, in your own community, to spread loving connections and support others? How can you make life better for those around you?

3. After reading this story, what does unvarnished faith mean to you? How can you be more intentional about practicing this in your own life?

4. Did any scene stick with you the most? What was it about that moment that was most meaningful? Are there other aspects of the story you particularly related to?

5. If given the chance, what would you like to ask Bill? Did anything come up that left you wanting to explore further?

6. What are three actionable takeaways for you—things you could start (or stop) doing now—after reading and discussing this book?

Author Q&A

Q: *What do you hope readers take away from this book?*

A: More than anything, I hope readers identify with some of the themes of the book such that they feel inclined to grow personally, professionally, or spiritually. I also hope they develop an appreciation (or greater appreciation) for the many blessings that so many of us have. Perhaps someone will be inspired to engage in mission work, either in a place like Nicaragua or in their local community . . . or maybe both!

Q: *How did you decide on character, dignity, talents, serenity, failure, and gratitude as your guiding themes? How did your life prior to the trip and how has your life since affirmed or challenged these themes?*

A: Writing the actual story of the mission was rather straightforward, even with the time and research required; this process was similar to the story writing I did in *Our Way*. What took far more time and energy was arriving at the six tenets that (for me) promote and nurture relationships and love. I didn't want to force-fit six concepts simply because the trip was six days long. The more I reflected on the trip and the more I read—I consumed over two dozen books about life, faith, and mission work—the more crystalized the six priorities became.

Looking at this process through a faith lens, I see it as a toggle between revelation and discernment: God reveals, I discern, God reveals more, I refine my discernment, and so on. I assume I miss(ed) many, if not most, of the messages God sends me, but I feel blessed to have received enough to land on the values in this book.

As far as my experiences before the trip, I incorporated in the text various anecdotes and learnings from my past that reinforce the book's messages. What has happened since settling on the list has been quite gratifying (yes, gratitude!): I have had almost weekly opportunities to discuss or pressure-test one or another of the themes. In virtually every instance, the words and descriptions I employed in the book have held up and, in some cases, perhaps helped someone else along their journey.

Q: *You are very aware of your privilege and preconceptions throughout this story. You acknowledge the white savior complex often associated with mission trips, and you didn't assume this trip would have a life-changing impact. Can you speak on this more?*

A: This trip took place before the pandemic and the associated amplified focus on privilege in many parts of America. As I worked on the book during the initial lockdown and concurrent calls for social and racial justice, I became unprecedentedly aware of the many blessings and privileges in my life. As I recounted the trip in these pages, I was routinely struck by the disparities and dichotomies between my world and life in Nicaragua. But I also discovered just as profoundly the foundational and visceral commonality that flows through all people. The juxtaposition of these realizations has indeed changed my life.

Q: *Your expression of Christianity as a contact sport is so powerful—the idea that you must be in motion and interacting with others to grow relationships. Central to this is touch. In the years since COVID-19, how has the* *isolation and distance affected this? Have you found other meaningful ways to grow relationships and spread love?*

A: I quoted Desmond Tutu at the start of the book. He is often associated with the African theological concept of *Ubuntu*, a term that means I exist because of you; I am a person only through how I relate to and interact with the rest of humanity and God's creation. This relationality has been altered and tested during the pandemic. On the one hand, I had unexpected months of time with my whole family under one roof. We watched the earth come to life on our daily walks, we planned out our meals well in advance, and we instituted weekly movie nights and pizza nights.

On the other hand, my connection with people beyond my direct family was severely curtailed. As a strong extrovert, this was challenging. Zoom certainly helped, as did the occasional outdoor, socially distanced gathering. One of the most profound lessons I learned during this time—and one of the greatest ways to express love and compassion—is simply telling another person, "I see you," letting them know that they matter and that I recognize and acknowledge them. I hope to carry this lesson well beyond today.

Q: *You write about the power of communication without words, the subtle way hugs and smiles can express so much love. What would you like to express to readers who may be struggling to communicate, whether in their own language or in learning a new one?*

A: How we communicate and interact is such a personal, intimate topic. I realize not everyone shares my affinity for touch . . . I am definitely a hugger! But a smile or a knowing, compassionate look into someone's eyes transcends age and race and gender and language and culture. We are social creatures. Our eyes and our facial expressions can be gateways into our souls and our commonality. My missionary experiences have ingrained in me how universally and lovingly we can connect with each other without ever saying a word.

Q: *You have a very poignant line: "So many Americans choose to be unhappy and complain, not in spite of our materialism but in light of it." What does unvarnished faith look like in an environment that is so hampered by material distractions? Have there been times since your experience in Nicaragua where you found yourself falling back into material trappings? How do you recognize this and remind yourself of your priorities?*

A: In highly developed parts of the world, not only is our faith *varnished*, but so is almost every other aspect of life—coated with layers of wealth, consumption, and luxury. And it's hard to crack through that varnish given that many people have not had the chance to immerse themselves in a totally different culture like I did in Pochocuape. How can someone be expected to have perspective on their life if all they have ever known is, well, their life? So I try not to judge or lecture.

And of course I, too, fall back into material trappings. I'd like to think, though, that through my mission work and writing this book, I am now at least more conscious of my lifestyle and surroundings and more dedicated to using what I have to promote the common good.

Q: *A beautiful theme throughout is the interplay of both physical and spiritual nourishment. Stepping away from the story, are you still able to see this in your daily life? Are there new ways you have continued to nurture this growth?*

A: This interplay continues to be a key balance in my life. In fact, through my recent graduate studies in ministry and theology, I have expanded on this two-part concept to a threefold approach to nourishment—physical, mental, and emotional—with the spiritual aspects of life enveloping all three. It is rare that we are able to attend sufficiently to all of these facets of our personhood, and the resulting imbalances show up in insidious and often debilitating ways. I believe these misalignments are a major outcome of the pandemic and the associated exponential growth in depression and anxiety in society. Conversely, when I am attentive to all three spheres, I become a much better version of myself.

Q: *You write about how you relate to the Serenity Prayer in three ways: that there are no coincidences, that you have grown to be comfortable in your own skin, and that you live in the moment. These are things that take time and practice to fully embody. Can you discuss what you found most helpful in your journey to get there?*

A: Among the book's tenets, serenity is the area in which I have experienced the most personal growth in recent years (with gratitude probably second). There is a concept in the counseling world called differentiation, which involves how effectively we know ourselves and how effectively we absorb, process, and react to people, situations, and inputs. One of the strongest areas of improvement I have achieved through a more intentional focus on my faith journey has been the ability to be comfortable with who I am and where I am in life—to be better differentiated. I feel more grounded and more aware of what my "true north" should be. Most importantly, I am trying to be more present, to be totally committed to the people and situations in front of me. This sounds so simple, but for me, it has been quite an effort to block out all the noise and busyness of life to prioritize the "who" and the "what" of right now.

Q: *A major piece of your section on serenity and indeed the concept of unvarnished faith is the peace that comes with trusting fully that God will provide what is needed for you and your loved ones to thrive. What would you say to secular readers or those who perhaps have less conviction in their faith?*

A: This is a good and important topic. While I live my life—and wrote this book—as a Christian, I hoped not to come across as an overzealous Bible thumper. I hoped to fill the proverbial canvas with enough relatable and universal stories and concepts so that followers of other faith traditions and people who choose not to practice faith could also derive value and perhaps inspiration for personal improvement.

I look forward to opportunities to discuss and debate *Unvarnished Faith*'s content with others. Our society is so polarized, with so much energy and agita directed toward the relatively few things that divide us. I believe it is principally through dialogue—the obsolescent but essential art of civil discourse—that the vitriol and animosity among us can dissipate.

Q: *As an author and speaker, one of your gifts is clearly a way with words. What was an early experience where you learned language has great influence?*

A: I always enjoyed writing and even public speaking as a boy and young adult. I then spent almost twenty-five years as a full-time businessperson, which routinely presented opportunities to write. I learned with my first book how different writing is in a corporate setting than in a book setting. In business, the approach is to tell them what you're gonna tell them, then tell them, then tell them what you told them. Writing a book is far more about storytelling, being intentional and often subtle about when and how various aspects of the narrative and characters and outcomes are revealed. I try to create compelling stories involving relatable people. And I try to create multisensory experiences where the reader does not just see but also hears, feels, and perhaps even smells and tastes what the characters are experiencing. It is all part of how art creates empathy, how a book or a play or a painting can foster connection and understanding.

Q: *Your first book,* Our Way, *is largely a memoir of your father's life. In writing* Unvarnished Faith, *did you notice any similarities or differences in the process? Do you have another book waiting in the wings?*

A: It is said that there are two paths for authors after publishing their first book. Some writers are content to have "checked the box" and opt to move on to their next challenge, like climbing a huge mountain or biking an enormous distance. I fell into a second category: I knew pretty much right away that I wanted to write another book. With *Our Way*, I learned so much about the writing process and had the chance to develop my craft. I was excited to begin the journey of this second book with these experiences and skills as a launching point.

I equate writing a book to painting a room. When engaging in the latter activity, the actual painting is the most important step. But there are several preceding tasks (color selection, material acquisition, room prep) and ensuing tasks (touch-up, drop cloth removal, outlet cover and drapery replacement). Similarly, the actual writing of the manuscript is the most critical step in producing a book. However, before you can put fingers to keyboard, you have to determine a general topic and theme, conduct extensive research, and develop a preliminary outline. Once the writing is mostly done, editing is a critical and time-consuming process, and then all the aspects of design, publication, and distribution kick in.

As far as future writing, I started composing original poetry during the pandemic; perhaps an anthology is in the offing. I am also curious to try my hand at fiction. My wife, Kelly, is a prolific reader and a mastermind at predicting plots of novels and television dramas. I'd love to collaborate with her on a book—one wherein even someone like her would struggle to predict the outcome.

About the Author

BILL YOH is an award-winning author, keynote speaker, business owner, and faith leader. Committed to the adage that the truly educated never graduate, he has earned master's degrees in business administration and in ministry and theology. Bill engages in service work in his local communities and abroad, employing and sharing the blessings of his talents, gifts, and resources. He lives with his family and their many pets in Pennsylvania and New Jersey. To learn more about unvarnished faith, find out when Bill is speaking next, and read some of his original poetry and other works, please go to www.unvarnishedfaith.com.

Made in the USA
Middletown, DE
07 February 2023

24155947R00158